ART COLLECTORS OF RUSSIA

THE PRIVATE TREASURES REVEALED

CHRISTINA BURRUS

with the collaboration of
AGNÈS CARBONELL

Photography by
LEONID OGAREV

Translated from the French by
ROS SCHWARTZ and SUE ROSE

TAURIS PARKE BOOKS, LONDON & NEW YORK

Acknowledgements

The author would like to thank the owners who have allowed their
collections to be reproduced in this book.

Art editor Peter Knapp
and page design by Véronique Rossi
Production by Raymond Lévy
assisted by Guylaine Cartron

© 1992 Sté Nouvelle des Éditions du Chêne
English translation © 1994 KEA Publishing Services Ltd., London
Published by Tauris Parke Books
45 Bloomsbury Square, London WC1A 2HY
in association with KEA Publishing Services Ltd., London

The Cataloguing in Publication Data for this book is available from the
British Library, London.

ISBN 1-85043-740-8

ENGLISH EDITION
Typesetting by Karen Stafford, DQP, 62 Cowcross Street, London EC1
Printed in France

Contents

Preface

Collecting is the only opportunity we have to exercise choice in a society which tends to standardize everything. This is the only way we can assert our independence.

Salomon Schuster

You can suffer and still have eyes for beauty.

Joseph Czapski

Glasnost, Perestroika... these words burst upon the world like a promise of renewal. I felt they had a magical quality and knew I could not rest until I could visit the country whose future was still uncertain, but which seemed to give free rein to our wildest hopes. I wanted to see it all, share it all, and give as much support as possible to the architects of this revolution. I saw the crowds gathered in front of the wall of photos depicting Stalin's victims. I visited the first retrospective of Pavel Filonov, a dissident painter. I went into re-opened churches, packed with believers and I met people who, until then, had lived in obscurity and silence. These encounters gave me the idea of giving western Europe the chance to discover the early work of a painter who is well-known here, although the paintings of his youth had never been seen: Marc Chagall. Private collections were opened, some magnificent paintings emerged from the reserve collections in various museums and the huge murals decorating the Kamerny State Jewish Theatre in Moscow could finally be restored. In the spring of 1991, I was one of 180,000 visitors to experience the shared exhilaration of this resurrection, made possible by the enthusiastic response of the Gianadda Foundation which provided a home for these masterpieces.

My research in connection with the Chagall exhibit meant that I made the acquaintance of the foremost collectors in the former Soviet Union. They welcomed me with open arms, giving me free access to the objects and canvases they had collected in semi-secrecy, sharing with me their incomparable wealth of expertise and their belief in the future.

There were so many discussions around samovars, and so many heart-stopping moments as well, when all of a sudden, above a bed or behind a door, I discovered a canvas by Petrov-Vodkin or Kuznetsov!

These were works which also deserved to be rescued from oblivion so they could bear witness to the rich artistic tradition of these countries, which seventy years of dictatorship could not wipe out.

In fact, after 1917, the only function of art was to glorify the proletarian forces and the Party's policies. Any attitude which the authorities judged anti-soviet resulted in deportation to the Gulag. On 19 September 1918, a decree was published prohibiting the export of works of art to other countries. These measures hit the private collectors even harder than the public institutions. The museums had no compunction about selling some of their treasures to meet the financial needs of the regime at the end of the twenties and at the beginning of the thirties. On 5 December 1918, a second decree simply abolished private collections, which then became State property. Shchukin and Morozov, the two major collectors of the time, had their possessions confiscated. The other collectors were forced to give the authorities an exhaustive list of the *objets d'art* in their possession. Their collections were placed under the protection of the State, which assumed total control of the administration of the 'Arts'. Some collectors, in exchange for a huge apartment, agreed to open their collections to the public. Others were regarded merely as custodians of the masterpieces they had collected or inherited. I should make it clear that citizens could only keep up with changes in the regulations by reading *Pravda*. Gradually, the idea of completely obliterating Russia's imperialist past came to be of paramount importance to the Soviet regime. Any reference to the years before the Revolution was censored. This policy, initiated at the beginning of the twenties, became increasingly intransigent and gave rise to the persecution which was to reach its peak in 1937, when Stalin came to power. The Stalinist period was the darkest of all for artists and intellectuals. At this time a canvas signed by Altman or Petrov-Vodkin could be bartered for next to nothing, or a family of deportees to the Gulag survive by disposing of antique objects or paintings which would become priceless. Naturally, abuse was widespread. Since everything belonged to the people, why go without? Certain museum curators took home works which were in their safe-keeping, neighbours absconded with canvases by the painter who was sharing a communal apartment with them, and the wholesale disposal of *objets d'art*, confiscated from their owners, was carried out at random. War made this situation even worse. Works vanished without trace, never to reappear. However, this confusion did enable the collectors to survive, albeit in semi-secrecy.

Shortly after the end of the war, Stalin agreed to the official return of most of the paintings which had been looted by the Soviet troops during the storming of Dresden. This goodwill gesture was short-lived: a sign of greater leniency, followed by a clamp-down by the Regime.

It was not until 1954, when Khrushchev came to power, that the thaw set in. The camps opened their gates, releasing an intelligentsia who had been given back their rights and were all now free to choose where they wanted to live. These former exiles, who had once more assumed full citizenship, actively supported Khrushchev's policies. A breath of liberalism swept across the USSR. Jeans were allowed, there were foreign broadcasts and American music on the radio. But this tolerant attitude was built on shaky ground. The first exhibition of modern art since the twenties was organized. Khrushchev put in an appearance at the opening ceremony, accompanied by an entourage of officials. Barely inside the door, he gave vent to a stream of coarse criticisms which would hardly do justice to an illiterate *moujik*, and spat on various paintings being exhibited. That was the end of the thaw as far as art was concerned. From then on, and for a long time after, exhibitions were held secretly in private apartments.

The practice of informing started up again with a vengeance. In exchange for a good room in a communal apartment or for some other benefit, people readily became informers. Brezhnev's regime, of the seventies, bequeaths a legacy of sinister memories. Emigration was the last bid for salvation. The country was emptied of its scholars and artists. Many Jews left, most often for the United States, via Vienna. Others obtained the status of political exiles. The dissidents, the internal political exiles, had to choose between leaving or being sent to the Gulag. The Russians still call these `the bulldozer years', in memory of the bulldozers sent by the masters of the Kremlin to demolish an art exhibition which was taking place in the street, and which, moreover, had been authorized. It was not until 1985, and Gorbachev's declaration of *Perestroika*, of greater openness, that people could breathe more easily. The stranglehold was loosened. But now that the initial enthusiasm has waned and the initial illusions have dissipated; it must be said that problems have got progressively worse. A breed of hitherto unknown collectors has appeared on the scene: the speculators. For them, art is a marketable commodity and they believe that a bank vault is the safest place to keep paintings. But, in a spirit of contradiction, the old system remains in force. All the collectors I met complained about the state of confusion which stands in the way of market development, and also works against the artists. Since the Union of Russian artists was dissolved, art galleries in London and Paris have welcomed them, but they are having difficulty adapting to the western market which is at times governed by the dictates of fashion. Russia's real problem, now as before, is its attitude towards the West. Should it imitate, come what may, a system with all too obvious failings and errors? Should it remain aloof, to preserve its national identity and protect the country from harmful influences? Since Peter the Great, the question has remained the same. Russia has always been torn between its fascination for western-style progress and its rejection of cultural imperialism. When looking at the ten collections illustrated in this book, readers will not only discover some neglected masterpieces, they will also come across characters who are living testaments to the recent past and to an evolutionary process with a disconcertingly rapid development . I have to admit that personal taste played a large part in determining the importance of these collections. I immediately eliminated many collectors whose hoarded acquisitions boast gemstones indiscriminately displayed with incomplete table services and where, occasionally, a bona fide masterpiece has the place of honour above the dining-room sofa, like a relic. I have selected collections which seemed to have an essential unity. They were all created after the Revolution and their owners, or their beneficiaries are still alive today. It is up to the reader to make up his own mind about the quality of these collections.

Personally, I would like to pay tribute to the courage, initiative and aesthetic judgement, to the love and scholarship of these men and women who are completely devoid of speculative or snobbish sentiments. Each of these collectors displays true greatness: that of having the sensitivity, taste and delicacy to be able to discern the intrinsic artistic truth in any creation. What would our museums and our memories be without them and without the spirit of initiative which prompted them to save part of our universal heritage?

CHRISTINA BURRUS

SHCHUKIN, MOROZOV, KOSTAKIS

Works of art are often condemned to an itinerant fate. In the past, the exodus of masterpieces was governed primarily by the hazards of conquests. The Italian wars or the Egyptian campaign are good examples. But, gradually, market forces replaced military vicissitudes. If it is now necessary to go to Moscow to admire some of Matisse's finest canvases, or Picasso's *L'Acrobate à la boule* (Young acrobat on a ball), this is because, at the turn of this century, two of the leading wealthy Russian patrons of the Parisian galleries were Sergei Shchukin and Ivan Morozov. In a little less than twenty years, between 1897 and 1914 to be precise, these two outstanding collectors transformed their Moscow homes into real museums of modern art. The passion for collecting was not new to Russia. Peter the Great had 'opened a window onto the West' by creating his capital, St Petersburg, out of nothing in the image of the European cities that he most admired. This window admitted all the fashions and foibles of London and Paris. Members of the aristocracy searched out bronzes, marbles and paintings fine enough to grace their mansions, which were copied from the ones owned by the nobility in Western Europe. Tsarina Catherine II instructed her ambassadors to purchase the paintings by Rubens, Rembrandt and Titian which are now the crowning glory of the Hermitage museum. Counts Stroganov and Sheremetev, as well as Prince Yusupov, vied with each other to outdo their sovereign's luxurious lifestyle. By the end of the eighteenth century, Russian collections were filled to overflowing with superb pieces. But, by the middle of the nineteenth century, the situation had begun to change. The aristocracy, attracted by the splendour of the past and fascinated by French and German court life, was replaced by members of a bourgeoisie who had acquired their wealth through trade. They were more aware of their Russian cultural heritage and more interested in innovation.

St Petersburg lapsed into splendid lethargy while Moscow asserted itself as the vital nerve-centre of the Empire. Shchukin and Morozov belonged to that generation of new collectors who relied more on their intuition than on traditional values. This audacity caused them to prefer Cézanne and Picasso to great works by earlier masters.

The Shchukin dynasty originally came from Borovsk, a small town situated to the west of Moscow. In the last years of the eighteenth century, one of the collector's ancestors owned the largest glassworks in the country. He employed German glass-blowers in his factories in the Ukraine and in Russia. The Napoleonic wars ruined him but the family's characteristic spirit of enterprise was passed down through the generations. A century later, Ivan Shchukin, the collector's father, was the owner of some prosperous textile factories. He was a very forceful personality, devoutly religious, and brought up his six sons the hard way. He sent them to a German school, in Vyborg, and entrusted them to the care of a Lutheran pastor who taught his pupils in accordance with the maxim 'a healthy mind in a healthy body'. However, although Ivan Shchukin was very strict with regard to the six brothers' personal expenditure, he never denied them the opportunity of travelling in France or Italy to develop their individual tastes.

All six caught the collecting fever which was wreaking havoc among the wealthy Russian bourgeoisie. The first to succumb was Piotr, the second eldest brother. During a stay in Germany, where he had been sent by his father to study factory procedures, he began to collect etchings and oriental artefacts, as well as photographs of famous artists. When he returned to Moscow, he became a frequent visitor to the Sukharev market, the Moscow flea market. Piotr rapidly accumulated an impressive collection (300,000 pieces) of Russian applied art. His modest wooden house soon became too small, so the young man took a long trip along the banks of the Volga in search of old buildings to serve as an inspiration for his new home. He took an architect with him who sketched out plans and studied the picturesque details of churches and wooden houses. He had not one house but two built on his return to Moscow, as his collection of objects had grown so large. These two houses, which were reminiscent of the famous wooden palace of Kolomenskoie, were connected by a tunnel, which housed his collection of furniture. One of the houses was devoted to objects of worship, icons and popular handicrafts. Sumptuous oriental rugs provided a setting for priceless table

1 **2**

Behind the façade of the former palace of the Trubetskoy princes,
the walls are covered with canvases which bear witness to the
unerring critical eye of the master of the house, Sergei Shchukin.

Portrait of Sergei Shchukin, around 1920.

3 **4**

Room devoted to The Rocks of Belle-Ile, *1886.*
Monet, in Sergei *Claude Monet.*
Shchukin's house, 1913. *Oil on canvas, 65 x 81 cm.*
Pushkin Museum, Moscow.

5

Piotr Shchukin's palace in Moscow, inspired by the famous wooden palace of Kolomenskoie, in 1910.

6

Piotr Shchukin's oriental room, housing works by Monet, Pissaro, Sisley and other French Impressionist artists.

7

OVERLEAF Rupé-Rupé *or* The Gathering of Fruits, *1899. Paul Gauguin. Oil on canvas. 130 x 190 cm. Pushkin Museum, Moscow*

13

services, silverware and simple everyday objects from bygone times. The walls were hung with hundreds of pieces of embroidery and Russian paintings dating from the eighteenth and nineteenth centuries. The other building housed a collection of manuscripts in an extraordinary library to which students were granted access.

In 1895, Piotr Shchukin opened his entire collection to the public. The accumulation of so many examples of Russian artistic genius was not merely an excuse for the patron to gratify his own personal predilections and slake his thirst for possession: he was also concerned with promoting national culture. His dearest wish was to turn his houses into museums. In 1905, this wish came true. The collector then adopted the role of curator and spent the last years of his life, until his death in 1912, watching over his treasures and showing them to visitors. In exchange for his donation, he was awarded the official title of State Councillor and wore his medals proudly. He dreamt of being given a title but had to be content with a lesser rank which meant that he finally qualified for a uniform which he wore daily, insisting that people call him 'Your Excellency'.

The third eldest Shchukin brother, Dimitri, specialized in western painting. Unlike Piotr, he did not have an ounce of snobbery in him, and family life was all that mattered to him. He had no time for honours and society functions. He studied economics in Dresden, but his sole interest was art. His naivety

and meekness made him easy prey for unscrupulous dealers, and many of his acquisitions turned out to be fakes. Against all odds, he bought several Dutch masterpieces, canvases by Vermeer, Metsu and Pieter de Hooch. The most famous of his paintings were the *Lamentation* by Rogier Van der Weyden and *The Music Lesson* by Gerard Ter Borch. Dimitri supplemented his Dutch collection with several examples of French eighteenth-century painting: works by Watteau, Boucher, Fragonard and Lancret. After the Revolution he sold the valuable manuscripts he had collected for next to nothing. His collection was nationalized in 1921 and became the museum of Early Western Art. He was appointed curator and carried out these duties until his death in 1932.

Two of the six brothers were destined to meet with a harsher fate. Vladimir and Ivan left Russia together for Paris in 1893. Vladimir died two years later in Biarritz at the age of twenty-seven. His loyal housekeeper, Fräulein Emma, was the only person who stayed with him and she brought his mortal remains back to Moscow. Ivan was undoubtedly the most eccentric member of the family. He adored Paris and settled there in style in the avenue de Wagram. His apartment quickly became a popular haunt for Russian artists and intellectuals in the capital. Life was lived to the full at this 'salon', where the interminable political and artistic discussions were not allowed to stand in the way of more sensual pleasures.

8

*Sergei Shchukin's dining-room,
devoted to Gauguin, in 1913.*

Ivan Shchukin and Rodin became firm friends and Shchukin also kept company with Degas and Renoir. One of his closest friends, the Spanish painter, Ignacio Zuloaga, introduced him to the splendours of Spanish art. Together with Rodin, the two aesthetes took a trip to Spain, following in the footsteps of El Greco, Goya and Zurburán. Shchukin bought various works and, in particular, several Goyas. But these outrageously extravagant purchases, in addition to his costly love affairs, finally ruined the family's prodigal son. Severely in debt, Ivan appealed to his brother Sergei who held the purse strings of the family fortune, but Sergei, who deeply disapproved of his brother's life of debauchery, remained obdurate. The young man was therefore forced to sell his Goyas, which turned out to be fakes. At his wits' end, Ivan Shchukin chose to commit suicide by poisoning himself. After his death, the sale of his collection covered only a quarter of his debts. The Ecole des Langues Orientales in Paris bought his collection of books, which is still one of its most valued collections.

Sergei was seemingly the most capable member of the clan. He took over the family textile business in 1890, leaving it only for periodic trips abroad. During a stay in Paris in 1897, one of his friends took him to the dealer Durand-Ruel in rue Laffitte in Paris. In this gallery, which was exhibiting work by the Impressionists, the merchant from Moscow fell in love with a painting by Claude Monet, *Lilas au soleil* (Lilacs of Argenteuil), which he immediately bought. This was to be the first Impressionist painting to enter Russia and the starting point of one of the most outstanding collections of this century. The former palace of the Trubetskoy Princes in the Manège quarter close by the Kremlin, where he lived in Moscow, soon became a temple of the avant-garde. Behind this façade, inspired by the late eighteenth-century fondness for neo-classicism, the walls were covered in canvases that revealed the unerring critical eye of the master of the house. His passion for the Impressionists lasted seven years. Thirteen Monets graced the music room and *Les Rochers de Belle-Ile* (Rocks of Belle-Ile), with its eddies of raging foam, hung next to two views of Rouen cathedral painted at different times of the day. The famous *Déjeuner sur l'herbe* (Luncheon on the grass), which Monet painted in homage to Manet, is the star of this collection. Beneath the heavily stuccoed ceilings, this huge canvas emanates the vivid dappled light of foliage filtered through undergrowth which reminded Shchukin and his guests of summers spent at the dacha.

Monet was not the only painter who enchanted Sergei Shchukin. He liked Sisley, Pissarro, Cézanne, from whom he bought eight paintings, and especially Gauguin. As his artistic sixth sense developed, the collector took more interest in contemporary painting. His tastes evolved slowly, from the Impressionists to the Post-Impressionists. His dining-room was devoted to Gauguin. Sixteen Tahitian views, hung in several rows, lined the walls of this massive room. The vibrant colours of flesh, palm trees, exotic flowers and fruit, unknown in Moscow, must have been impressive

9

*Sergei Shchukin's pink room,
with works by Matisse, in 1913.*

in the half-light created by heavy drapes. This dazzling display was in marked contrast to the formality of the decor, the enormous chandeliers and rococo furniture. Shchukin bought his most famous Gauguins from Ambroise Vollard: *Rupé-Rupé* or *La Cueillette des fruits*, (The gathering of the fruits) and *Te avae no Maria* or *Le Mois de Marie* (Tahitian woman with flowers). These paintings, sent by the painter from Tahiti, had embarked on an incredible journey. Leaving a distant island, they had arrived at Vollard's picturesque shop in rue Laffitte to travel on to grace the Trubetskoy Palace. If what André Salmon says is true, Vollard was, 'the most discriminating, the most intelligent' of art dealers, but also 'the most slovenly'. To acquire these treasures, Shchukin did not consider it beneath him to 'sweep and dust this Aladdin's cave', this 'pigsty where you might extract one of those superb Cézannes from under a rickety sideboard, while Vollard was having lunch in his cellar, napkin tucked under his chin and a Renoir propped up in front of him'.

After Gauguin, Shchukin conceived an enthusiasm for Henri Matisse, who was a little-known artist at the time. It was probably at the house of Berthe Weil, the painter's original dealer, that the Russian art lover saw his still lifes with their bright colours and bold technique. This was also a Bohemian setting, as Berthe Weil not only sold paintings but also books and second-hand goods. Shchukin liked Matisse's works so much that he lost no time in visiting him at his studio on the quai Saint-Michel. The artist

himself recounted how the collector noticed a still life hanging on the wall and said: 'I am going to buy it, but I must have it at home for several days first and if I can stand it and it still interests me, I will keep it'. 'I was fortunate,' added Matisse, 'that he was able to survive that first ordeal quite easily, and that my still life didn't bore him too much.' So, as early as 1904, Shchukin's collection included two oils by Matisse. This initial visit blossomed into a firm friendship. There was a great deal of truth in the view that the Russian was the ideal patron for the painter. In 1909 he commissioned two large panels to decorate the staircase of his palace. *La Danse* (Dance) and *La Musique* (Music), major twentieth-century works, were the direct result of this meeting between the bourgeois Muscovite and the painter from the Mediterranean. The two compositions were actually inspired by the quality of light in the South of France: 'When I started *La Danse* and *La Musique,* commissioned by Shchukin, I was determined to use colours without any shading or depth. I knew that my musical chord was represented by a green and a blue (representing the relationship between the green pines and the blue sky of the Côte d'Azur) along with another colour for the flesh of the figures.' Matisse emphasized the importance of the Mediterranean inspiration for *La Danse*: 'The original and chief structural element of this composition was rhythm; the second was a great expanse of intense blue (reference to the Mediterranean sky in August); the third was a green mound (the green of Mediterranean pines against

10

One of the rooms in
Sergei Shchukin's palace, in 1913

11

Harmony in Red, *1908-9.*
Henri Matisse. Oil on Canvas. 180 x 220 cm.
Hermitage Museum, St Petersburg.

the blue sky).' When he was completing this commission, the painter had not seen the house he was designing it for, but the setting influenced his work from afar: 'I have to decorate a staircase. There are three floors. I picture the visitor coming in from outside. The first floor beckons to him. He must be encouraged to make an effort, be made to feel lighter. My first panel represents dance, that ecstatic ring of dancers on the hilltop. On the second floor, you are inside the house; its spirit and silence suggest a musical scene with people listening; finally on the third floor, there is total tranquillity and I will paint a restful scene: people lying on the grass, chatting or day-dreaming.' Only the first two stages of this plan were executed for Shchukin and exhibited at the Salon d'Automne of 1910, before being sent to Moscow, where they arrived in 1911. People flocked to Znamensky Street to view the latest creations by the collector's protégé. The following year, the journal *The Golden Fleece* devoted an entire issue to Matisse, who had become the most famous western painter in Russia. Then, in the autumn of 1911, Matisse finally accepted Shchukin's pressing invitation and visited Moscow, which he thought resembled 'a huge Asian village'. This fortnight-long stay made a great impact both on the painter and his public. The artist became passionately interested in icons which, in his opinion, 'ranked alongside the work of the French primitives'. The young up-and-coming practitioners of Russian painting avidly absorbed the lessons of the master, to such an extent that Valentin Serov, a famous portrait painter and professor at the Academy of Fine Arts in Moscow, wrote with a certain bitterness: 'After this spicy fare, school food is insipid, there is nothing for it but to give up teaching, because [young painters] do not want to listen any more, they are all "concocting" their own recipes and are refusing to learn.'

From the year before, some of the ring leaders of the new generation, whose lack of discipline was deplored by Serov, had earned the nickname of 'Russian Matisses'. They included

12 13

20

Dance, *1910. Henri Matisse.*
Oil on Canvas. 260 x 391 cm.
Hermitage Museum, St Petersburg.

Music, *1910. Henri Matisse.*
Oil on Canvas. 260 x 389 cm.
Hermitage Museum, St Petersburg.

14

Antique market,
Sukharev Square in Moscow.

15

The conversation, 1909. Henri
Matisse. Oil on canvas. 177 x 217 cm.
Hermitage Museum, St Petersburg.

21

Laryonov, Goncharova, and Konchalovsky, who were regular visitors to the rooms on Znamensky Street, which were generously opened to the public by their owner.

La Danse and La Musique were not only revelations for the Russian public. Even their creator found that his reunion with them after several months was an unexpected surprise. 'In Moscow, I was extremely interested to have another look at that canvas [La Danse] after being away from it. Contrary to what I had thought when I was creating it – that only the arrangement of the coloured areas, irrespective of the material, would convey the overall impression of the work – I realized that my material had its own importance and that the richness of the painting is greatly enhanced by the brushwork which allows the brilliance of the white canvas to show through, and transforms these flat colours into dynamic areas: a sort of shimmering, mottled effect.' Distance in time and space gave the work new and unsuspected layers of meaning, and enabled Matisse to see these canvases in a different light; canvases which, a long way from his Parisian studio, provided fresh inspiration both for the Russian avant-garde and his own genius.

At Shchukin's house, the pink room was devoted to the painter of La Danse. In 1914, the collection comprised thirty-seven paintings. They included Les Poisson Rouges (Goldfish or The Red Fish), whose dazzling colours and naive technique were in brazen contrast to the ostentatious ceilings and the Louis XV armchairs: La Chambre Rouge, also called La Desserte, harmonie rouge (The Red Room or Harmony in Red) with its blue arabesques against a crimson background, is reminiscent of the stylized motifs found on oriental rugs. But it was in his dining-room, with his Gauguins, that Shchukin was to hang one of his last acquisitions, the immense Conversation. For many years he had coveted this canvas, which Matisse eventually gave to him. 'I think about your blue painting with two figures a great deal', wrote the collector. And this huge composition, representing two motionless hieratic figures, caught for ever, mid-conversation, certainly had everything it took to entrance Shchukin, who was an admirer of Egyptian antiquities. Although Claude Monet was his first love, he had in time become more fascinated by works whose powerful forms reminded him of the ancient sculptures which he would always go to see at the Louvre on his trips to Paris. He liked to recognize silhouettes from ancient Egypt behind Cézanne's peasants. The primitive majesty of Gauguin's Tahitian women and Matisse's strict musicality deeply satisfied this 'extremely sober' man who, according to Matisse, only enjoyed 'calm, serious pleasures'.

So it was not surprising that he developed a great enthusiasm for the work of Pablo Picasso, from whom he bought fifty-one paintings between 1909 and 1914. For this new favourite, the merchant abandoned the over-blown decor of his home. He hung his Picassos in a small, vaulted and completely white room, which he called his cell. Only the monastic simplicity of this room could provide a suitable setting for the Spaniard's canvases, which were characterized by an imposing sense of melancholy. Shchukin

16

PREVIOUS PAGE LEFT Woman with a fan, *1909.*
Pablo Picasso. Oil on canvas. 101 x 81 cm.
Pushkin Museum, Moscow.

17

PREVIOUS PAGE RIGHT Woman holding a fan
(After the ball) *1908. Pablo Picasso.*
Oil on canvas. 150 x 100 cm.
Hermitage Museum, St Petersburg.

18

'White room'
in Sergei Shchukin's palace,
devoted to Picasso.

19

The absinthe drinker, *1901.*
Pablo Picasso.
Oil on canvas. 73 x 54 cm.
Hermitage Museum, St Petersburg.

24

owned several of the masterpieces from the rose and blue periods. One of the paintings from the latter period, the *Portrait de Sabartès* (Portrait of Jaime Sabortès) dating from 1901, is described by the writer who sat for his friend: 'I look at myself, I see myself caught on the canvas and justify what I suggested in response to my friend's anxiety: this is the ghost of solitude, seen from the outside... a fabulous blue mirror. It is as if the vast surface of a lake has retained a part of me because I can see my reflection in it.' Most of the collection, however, belongs to the Cubist period which followed the two monochrome periods. Shchukin was also a frequent visitor to the gallery owned by Kahnweiler, a young German who had settled in Paris in 1907 and who had sold him most of the twenty-nine Cubist Picassos that he owned, including the famous *Dame à l'éventail* (Woman with a fan). In the white cell, among the 'intruders' which were not by Picasso, there was the *Portrait d'Apollinaire et de sa muse* (Marie Laurencin: The Muse Inspiring the Poet) by the Douanier Rousseau. For a long time, this work confounded its owner, who nonetheless ventured to buy seven canvases by this unclassifiable painter. He was probably attracted by the forceful presence of the figures and by the bold colours which were a little reminiscent of Gauguin.

Finally, loyal to the Fauves, who included Matisse in his early years, Shchukin was fond of André Derain. These cleanly-

executed paintings, which look as if they have been carved out of a frozen landscape, enabled the collector to rediscover the purity of line and the measured rhythms which he most valued.

But the turbulent course of history regained the upper hand. Several months after the October Revolution Sergei Shchukin left Russia and settled in Paris. His family had been hit by adversity: two of his sons had committed suicide. The third was studying the history of Persian and Indian art at the Sorbonne. He was to become an archeologist. At the end of the twenties, the Soviet government attempted to solve its financial problems by selling some paintings which had belonged to former private collections. Shchukin protested, stating that he had collected these works for the people and he refused to retrieve his property in this way. He died in France in 1936. In 1954, Moscow loaned several of his Picassos to an exhibition in Paris. Shchukin's daughter asked the French government to sequester these canvases but she lost her case and her father's Picassos returned to Russia, never to leave the country again.

The Morozov family made its fortune in the textile industry. The two brothers, Mikhail (1870-1903) and Ivan (1871-1921), shared a passion for collecting. The eldest was a self-styled man of letters and art critic. He was primarily interested in modern western painting, but nevertheless did not neglect Russian art. He

lived in a private mansion on boulevard Smolensky which was described some years later by Maurice Denis as 'a Pompeian, Egyptian, Moorish house', a 'distinctive string of rooms decorated with figures from hypogea, amorous couples from Pompeii, and heroes by Flaxman'. It was in this setting, and especially in the winter garden, that Mikhail Morozov hung precious icons, Russian *fin-de-siècle* canvases and the leading names in French painting such as Gauguin, Renoir, Toulouse-Lautrec and Degas Isaak Levitan and Vrubel, 'a kind of satanic Gustave Moreau' according to Maurice Denis, were hung next to Corot and the Impressionists. The finest piece in the collection was the portrait of the actress, Jeanne Samary, by Renoir. The young woman is a dazzling vision of delicate, red-haired beauty. The white dress she is wearing may have inspired some of the outfits favoured by Mikhail's wife, Margarita Morozova, who was renowned for her elegance. In 1903, Mikhail died at the age of thirty-three. His widow bequeathed the collection to the Tretyakov Gallery in 1910. But his brother, Ivan, had taken over where he left off: in 1903, he bought his first foreign painting, *La Neige à Louveciennes* (The Snow at Louveciennes), by Alfred Sisley.

If Mikhail felt that he was a born writer, Ivan was a painter by vocation. He studied with Konstantin Korovin, a francophile who was greatly influenced by the Impressionists and who liked to paint pictures of places he dreamt of such as Parisian boulevards at dusk and shady avenues in Provençal towns. Influenced by his elder brother's predilections and by his lessons with his professor, Ivan Morozov conceived two passions: modern

26

20 · 21 · 22 · 23

TOP, FROM THE LEFT The Morozov brothers in a villa near Moscow. First from the right, Alexis, collector, founder of the Porcelain Museum in Moscow; second from the right, Ivan. Around 1910.

BOTTOM LEFT The actress Jeanne Samary, 1878. Pierre-Auguste Renoir. Oil on canvas. 173 x 103 cm. Hermitage Museum, St Petersburg.

BOTTOM RIGHT Mikhail Morozov next to the Paris–Moscow train, 1902.

OPPOSITE On the right, Margarita Morozova in front of the portrait of her deceased husband Mikhail, painted in 1903 by Valentin Serov. Seated, her three children, Iriy, Helène and Mika.

24

Ivan Morozov's private mansion,
Pretchistenka Street in the centre of Moscow.

25

Staircase in Ivan Morozov's home,
housing the triptych by Bonnard,
The Mediterranean.

28

26

The Mediterranean, *triptych, 1911.*
Pierre Bonnard. Oil on canvas.
LEFT-HAND PANEL *407 x 149 cm.*
CENTRAL PANEL *407 x 152 cm.*
RIGHT-HAND PANEL *407 x 149 cm.*
Hermitage Museum, St Petersburg.

27
Mount St.Victoire, *1900.*
Paul Cézanne. Oil on canvas. 78 x 99 cm.
Hermitage Museum, St Petersburg

painting and Paris and at the time these two things were synonymous. Instead of becoming an artist, he became a collector in a class of his own. Everything about this man, whom Matisse called 'the Russian colossus' was huge: his build, his fortune, which enabled him to spend 300,000 francs each year on buying works of art and his home, a palace on Prechistenka Street in Moscow. The first floor was devoted to his collection. Naturally, the Impressionists were widely represented by some hundred canvases, but there were also the finest Cézannes, Van Goghs and a great number of Gauguins. These rooms 'with the simple, large and heavy pieces of furniture in understated shades of grey', were lined with apparently disparate choices, linked nonetheless by a discernible guiding principle. Colour was the dominant theme of the Morozov collection. The furniture merely acted as a foil for the brilliant paintings that the patron loved so much. All the rooms contained huge bunches of lilacs, lily of the valley and cyclamen, their muted colours accentuating the vivid harmonies of the Cézannes and the Bonnards. These two painters were among Morozov's favourites; in particular, he had an unfaltering passion for Cézanne. Unlike Shchukin, who liked the Provençal artist's eternal figures caught in timeless poses, Morozov much preferred Cézanne's brighter canvases. *Les Pommes jaunes* (Yellow Apples), *La Leçon de piano* (The Piano Lesson), *Le Paysage bleu* (Blue Landscape) with their pure vibrant colours attracted him more than Cubism's pioneering system of symbols. Legend had it that Morozov left blank places on his walls which he would not fill until he had found the painting with the exact shading he had envisaged

for that spot. He put his collection together like a giant palette and became very enthusiastic about the Nabis, a group of painters formed in 1892 by members of Académie Julien in Paris. Bonnard's lyricism, which transformed familiar scenes into glorious symphonies, appealed to him to such an extent that he commissioned three panels from the painter to decorate the main staircase in his private mansion. Between the stately neo-classical columns, the triptych *La Méditerranée* (The Mediterranean) flaunted its iridescent colours like a stained-glass window, brightening the Russian greyness with a touch of southern light.

Morozov appreciated large-scale works, immense decorative designs. He gave Maurice Denis, his favourite artist, the task of decorating his music room. In 1908 Denis painted *L'Histoire de Psyché* (The story of Psyche), inspired by a recent trip to Mantua where he saw the frescos by Giulio Romano at the Palazzo del Te. 'The *Psyche* room outshines everything,' he wrote, 'it represents the triumph of painting and of sensuality in painting. There is splendour, the reification of human beings, inordinate paganism, Psyche and Eros in bed.' But the Moscow work is worlds apart from this unbridled sensuality. In contrast to Giulio Romano's nudes, Maurice Denis painted chaste ethereal figures, belonging to a purely spiritual system of symbols. When he stayed in Russia, the artist found that his work was 'somewhat isolated in a huge chilly room, stone-grey with mouse-coloured furniture'. He remarked 'that it needed something to CONNECT'. And he advised Morozov to commission four bronzes from Aristide Maillol, based on the four seasons. The patron took this advice, just as he was happy to follow

28

Café at Arles, *1888. Paul Gauguin.*
Oil on canvas. 72 x 92 cm.
Hermitage Museum, St Petersburg.

29

OVERLEAF Peaches and pears, *1888-90.*
Paul Cézanne. Oil on canvas. 61 x 90 cm.
Hermitage Museum, St Petersburg.

31

that of the dealers and the critics whom he visited. Unlike Shchukin, who bought anything he liked on impulse, Morozov was more cautious and heedful of expert opinion. 'When Morozov visited Ambroise Vollard, he would say: "I want to see a very fine Cézanne". Whereas Shchukin would ask to see all the Cézannes and make his own choice.' This account by Matisse provides an insight into the very different personalities of the two collectors.

Shchukin appeared to have a completely personal approach, while Morozov was more influenced by what he saw around him, a feeling, a new opinion, the mood of the times. At Shchukin's home, in Znamensky Street, the rooms were arranged in ideal groupings: Gauguin in the dining-room, Matisse in the pink room, Picasso in his cell. However, at Prechistenka Street, the arrangement of canvases, despite displaying certain affinities, was questionable in its apparent disorder. Maurice Denis commented that one of the panels from his *Histoire de Psyché* was placed 'between some Cézannes and some Tahitian Gauguins'. And he added: 'Cézanne shows me up, yes, but Gauguin is really not that much better than me.' These eclectic settings did have a certain piquant charm, which stemmed from the contrasts generated: 'I am influenced as much by Italian and French forms as by oriental colours and rug patterns'. In another part of the exhibition the same subject united two very different canvases: 'The two *Café d'Arles* (Cafe at Arles), the one by Gauguin with the woman from Arles, the bottle and the smoke, dark and well crafted; the other by Vincent, glowing and totally distorted, but with so much feeling, so full of life that it makes the Gauguin look pedantic'.

Shchukin and Morozov did, however, share certain passions: for Matisse as well as Cézanne. Morozov acquired eleven canvases by Shchukin's friend Matisse, among which the most striking are those which make up the *Triptyque marocain: Zorah sur la terrasse, Vue de la fenêtre* and *La Porte de la Casbah* (Moroccan Triptych: Zorah on the terrace, Window at Tangiers, Entrance to the Casbah), which were painted in Tangiers in 1912. This purchase gave Matisse another opportunity to tackle an issue that was dear to his heart: the framing of his works. It is a surprise, nowadays, to see such daring canvases in their heavy old-fashioned frames, whose gilding seems terribly ostentatious, completely out of harmony with Cézanne and Picasso's dazzling modernity. Matisse was aware of this incompatibility: 'Paintings or drawings,' he wrote, 'depending on exactly where they are hung, must be in perfect harmony with the frame, in the same way as a recital of chamber music will take into consideration the dimensions of the room where it is to be heard.' In a letter to Morozov, dated 13 April 1913, he gave him some further advice about the frames for the *Triptyque marocain*: 'The frames have been designed with the paintings in mind and are grey. They were painted with size. You can remove any smudges made by fingerprints by gently wiping them away with a slightly damp cloth'. Matisse even went so far as to detail his recipe, in case the frames needed to be repainted: 'This grey is created by mixing whiting or another powdered white, a little black and a little ultramarine and some gelatin to seal it.' The restraint of the end result perfectly matched what we know of the interior of Morozov's

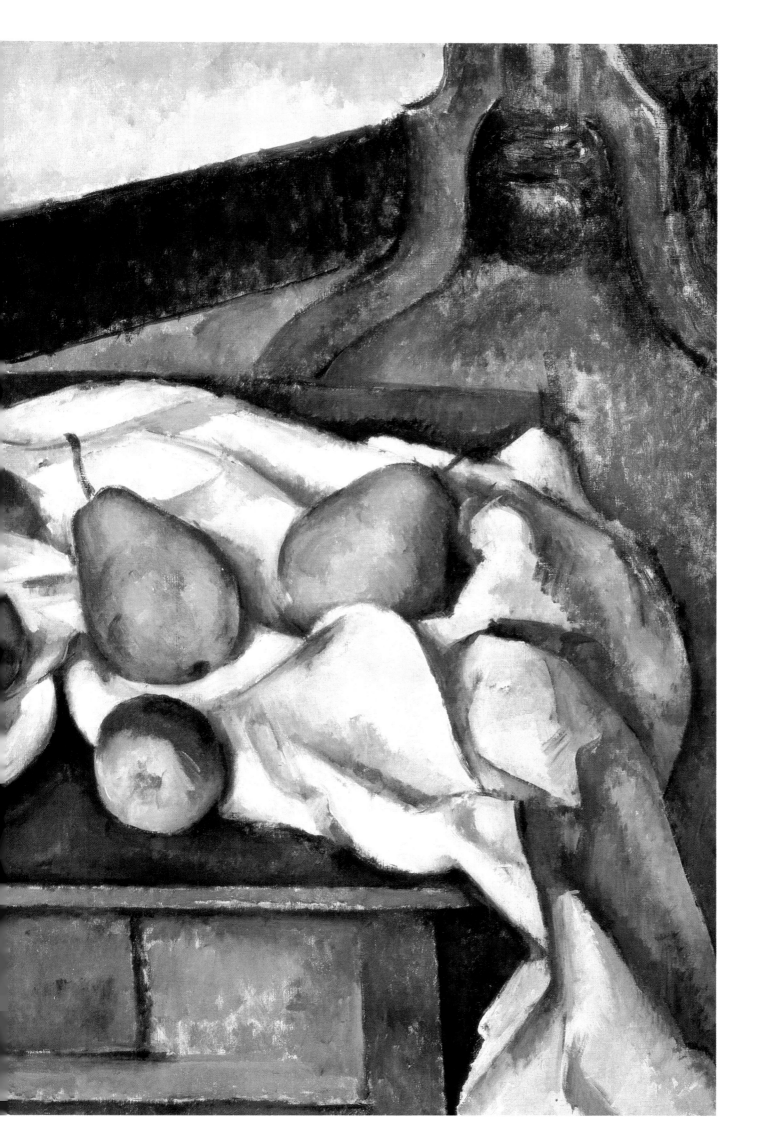

30 - 31

PREVIOUS PAGES Moroccan Triptych, *1912.*
Henri Matisse. RIGHT-HAND PANEL Entrance to the
Casbah, *oil on canvas, 115 x 80 cm.*
CENTRAL PANEL Zorah on the terrace. *Oil on canvas.*
115.8 x 100.5 cm. Hermitage Museum, St Petersburg.

32

The hairdressing salon (Uncle Zussy), *1914.*
Marc Chagall.
Gouache and oil on paper, 49.3 x 37.2 cm.

33

Young Acrobat on a ball, *1905.*
Pablo Picasso.
Oil on canvas. 147 x 95 cm.
Pushkin Museum, Moscow.

house and set off the sumptuous colours of these Moroccan views. With Shchukin, however, the over-blown decorative appearance of the frames, whose gold tones gleam like an iconostasis in the gloom, is still surprising. But this incongruity had for Morozov its own rationale, as we have seen.

Shchukin's admiration for Picasso also influenced Morozov. He bought three of his paintings, including the portrait of the dealer, Ambroise Vollard and the famous *Young Acrobat on a ball*, one of the masterpieces from the rose period. In a landscape reduced to several coloured bands, two travelling acrobats face each other. The little girl standing on a ball and the huge man sitting on a cube both seem to be sharply etched onto the canvas. This severity is mitigated by the sophisticated rose and blue shadings, which boast an unusual delicacy.

On the eve of the War, Russian artists could admire the output of the western avant-garde, either at Morozov's home or at Shchukin's home. Interviewed in 1920 by the critic Félix Fénéon, Ivan Morozov explained that his collection was not solely there for his own personal enjoyment: 'At the time of the Tsars, anyone who was interested could visit my house on Sunday mornings, and, provided they observed a few formalities which were hardly unreasonable, artists and critics could come and see my home any other day except Monday.' In reply to Fénéon's question regarding the painters most favoured by Russian artists, he said: 'Cézanne. I had twenty examples of his genius on display: two *Montagne Sainte-Victoire* (Mount St. Victoire), *La Leçon de piano,* one *Jas de Bouffan,* a portrait of his wife, among others. Van Gogh was also greatly admired. And Derain. And Picasso, but I only had three of his canvases. Both he and Henri Matisse were more widely represented at Mr Shchukin's house.'

The personal museums kept by these two exceptional collectors became breeding grounds of ideas for Russian painters at the beginning of this century. They had a profound effect on the minds of the artists who were soon to challenge the very premises of art: it was no longer a decorative, elitist activity, but a popular practice dealing with every aspect of daily life. The War and the Revolution cut Russia off from Europe. The constant flow of paintings and ideas which linked the Tsarist Empire with western Europe ceased. Morozov turned back to Russian painting and bought canvases by Levitan, Vrubel, Korovin, his former teacher, and Somov. In 1919, his collection nationalized and his palace transformed into a museum, he went into exile. He died two years later in Karlsbad, at the age of fifty.

In 1917, during the Russian interim government, France sent two left-wing deputies, Marius Moutet and Marcel Cachin on an official visit to Russia. They asked to see the Shchukin and Morozov collections. The former received them warmly but the latter refused, on the pretext that his paintings were in crates ready for his departure from Moscow. After seeing Shchukin's collection, Moutet wrote, not without irony: 'What a pity that our bourgeoisie missed out on all these treasures! We are indebted to the Russian bourgeoisie for saving these masterpieces of western modern art.' At the beginning of 1918, the Bolsheviks gave orders that private collections were to be confiscated. The works were left in the houses of the two patrons. By 1933, the Morozov and Shchukin collections had been amalgamated into one collection within the Museum of Western Art, which was housed in Morozov's palace. The names of the former owners were eventually removed from all museum publications, and from all the legends of the paintings. As Romain Rolland wrote in the museum's visitors' book, during his visit to Russia: 'Wandering through the rooms of this wonderful museum, I was surprised and moved to rediscover some of the finest canvases that had enchanted me in my youth. Renoir, the early work of Claude Monet and Cézanne, whom Vollard had possessively hidden in his shops. That rich period of French art, one of the most glorious periods in painting, was there before my very eyes. I am glad to see that this collection of riches, this French symphony, is flourishing under the USSR's

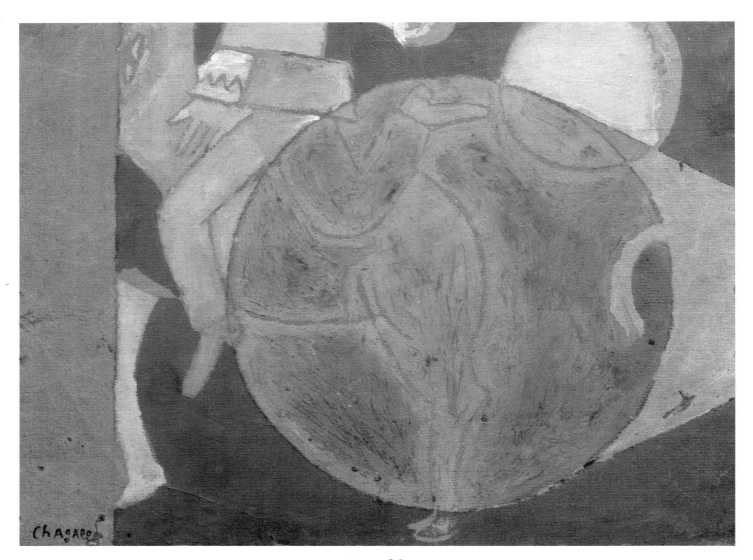

34

*The Circus, 1919. Marc Chagall. Oil on paper
stuck on canvas. 31.3 x 41.3 cm. Private collection.*

friendly auspices.' There was no mention of Shchukin or Morozov. Romain Rolland probably knew how Soviet Russia had obtained this extraordinary collection of masterpieces, but as a loyal friend of the authorities, he preferred to forget it.

It was not until some twenty years after Shchukin and Morozov went into exile that a humble embassy employee, a Greek by the name of George Kostakis, once more took up the torch lit by his renowned predecessors. If they were the ones who had incited a true artistic revolution in Russia by allowing young painters at the beginning of the century to discover and examine closely the works of Cézanne or Picasso, Kostakis was responsible for a definitive shift in the way that western Europe regarded modern Russian art.

George Kostakis was the third child of a Greek merchant living in Moscow and was born there in 1912. Although his social background was completely different from that of his seniors, he shared their innate talent for being able to spot a masterpiece out of hundreds of paintings. He had the 'sixth sense', the unerring eye of great collectors. He began, in the thirties, by collecting Russian silverware from the sixteenth and seventeenth

centuries. At that time, he was employed as a driver for the Greek delegation in Moscow. He stayed there until 1943, when he joined the Canadian Embassy as head of supplies and soon became personnel manager. He stayed until 1978, the year of his permanent departure for Greece. He supplemented his silver collection with porcelain, precious Caucasian rugs and some forty Flemish and German canvases. His salary, paid partly in foreign currencies and partly in food coupons, enabled him to assuage his passion.

Throughout these years, the Greek immigrant's son cherished the dream of climbing the social ladder, which would finally enable him to dine with the diplomats at black-tie affairs and be on the same footing as people like Shchukin and Morozov. At the end of the war, an inspired hunch prompted him to resell all his antiques and direct his attentions to Russian painting from the period 1913-23. The combination of circumstances was propitious. No-one had dared show an interest in this genre of art which Stalin had labelled decadent. The collector then gave free rein to that formidable business sense inherited from generations of oriental merchants. He had no compunction in exploiting the misfortune and poverty of families of artists who had been exiled or who had

35
George Kostakis

39

disappeared. At one point he even swapped some aspirin for a magnificent canvas. In this way, he acquired various Kandinskys, Chagalls, Malevichs and soon owned the largest collection of Russian modern art. But pride in his possessions was not enough for George Kostakis. He wanted to be acknowledged. As it was difficult for people to make a name for themselves in the USSR, he was to do it through the West. Due to his numerous contacts in the diplomatic world, he was able to get certain paintings out of the country. Western Europe was unprepared for its introduction to the qualities of Russian painting and to Kostakis himself. On one occasion Kostakis showed one of Chagall's earliest masterpieces, *Le Cirque* (The Circus), in which a green sphere inscribed in a pink rectangle spins men and animals round and round, up and down, in a cosmic carnival. Another delivery by diplomatic bag produced Malevich and El Lissitzky, whose aggressive geometric forms seemed to be inspired by the Bauhaus slogan 'less is more'. Finally, in 1953, George Kostakis, following the example of S. Shchukin and I. Morozov, opened his collection to young Soviet artists. He had arrived, but despite frequent trips abroad, he was not his own man. In 1973, on his return from a trip to the United States, he considered emigrating. His network of contacts protected him, but

not enough to prevent his dacha in Bakova from being burgled in 1974. From then on, the collector began to make arrangements for his permanent departure from the USSR. It took five years of negotiations to obtain his freedom in exchange for half of his collection. He settled in Rome in 1978, then in Kifisia, near Athens, where he died in 1991.

Like Sergei Shchukin and Ivan Morozov, George Kostakis acted as a link between Russia and western Europe. But his influence was in the opposite direction. The two collectors from pre-revolutionary Russia introduced their country to the greatest modern artists in the West. Kostakis, on the other hand, introduced Russian painters, who had absorbed the lessons of Cézanne, Matisse and Picasso with genius, to the countries on the other side of the Iron Curtain. One might say that without Shchukin and Morozov, several of the collections in this book might not have existed, since they were created around the works of various painters who, between 1910 and 1920, had extended, and were not merely subject to, the cardinal influence of these foreign models. Without George Kostakis, we would be less prepared for the visual impact of so many masterpieces, less able to understand their historical significance or grasp their stunning modernity.

36

Proun JC., *1919. Lazar Lissizky.*
Oil and collage on wood. 67.5 x 67.5 cm.
Tretyakov Gallery, Moscow.

40

37
Red Square.
Kazimir Malevich.
Gouache on lined paper, 61 x 57 cm.
Tretyakov Gallery, Moscow.

38
Black square.
Kazimir Malevich.
Oil on canvas. 24 x 17 cm.
Tretyakov Gallery, Moscow.

SALOMON A. SCHUSTER'S COLLECTION

1

Behind the drawn curtain, the collection becomes a stage set. On this imaginary stage, past and present swap roles. The collector, now a magician, breathes life into the works around him and gives the apparent diversity of the collection a mysterious unity, of which he alone holds the secret.

Salomon Abramovich Schuster was born in 1934 and is the son and grandson of collectors. In his apartment, the first room that the visitor enters is the bedroom, in which several seventeenth and eighteenth-century French canvases are hung: vestiges of his father, Abram Ignatievich Schuster's collection. These remnants of one of the most famous collections of western European paintings in Russia are a prelude to another Schuster collection, that of Salomon, which was devoted to Russian artists from the first half of the twentieth century. The family collection was broken up many years ago, and housed in different museums. At the beginning of the fifties, when Salomon Schuster was beginning to acquire Russian works deemed too formalist by the authorities, his father was being forced to part with his treasures at rock-bottom prices.

'My father lived in a lonely apartment, filled with penitent Mary Magdalenes, apostles and prophets. He had severe money problems, but only confided in a few friends. He would eat his meagre meals on a magnificent seventeenth-century Swedish table. Occasionally he would sell one of his paintings and this is how the Hermitage acquired a superb Caspar David Friedrich, *Landscape with figures*, for a ridiculously low price. The best Russian canvases in his collection were bought by the Russian museum of St Petersburg, in particular two works by Borovikovsky, the famous *Portrait of Levitsky* and *David singing Psalms*.'

When his father died, Salomon Schuster wanted to put a stop to this erosion of the collection and gave the Hermitage virtually all that remained of it. He felt that the finest paintings by

2

'My family has lived in St Petersburg since 1928. My great-grandfather was in charge of town lighting. My father, who was an architect, was devoted to preserving the harmony of this town whose geometric precision is tempered by the proximity of the sea and by the golden domes reflected in countless canals.'

Pittoni, Palmarolli, Batoni and Hogarth, should be brought together under one roof, to continue to bear witness, room after room, to the personality of those who had once collected them. But contrary to the express request of the benefactor, most of the canvases remained in the museum's reserve collection, consigned to oblivion just as a second collection began to make a name for itself. If there is a heritage, it is more that of a tradition, a state of mind, than the possession of tangible objects. The collection that Salomon Schuster built up ran counter to that of his father. He preferred portraits by Robert Falk and Martiros Saryan to repentant Magdalenes and he abandoned western painting for the charms of the Orient. The first work that he bought, at the age of twelve, was a seventeenth or eighteenth-century Chinese vase.

Within five years, with his father's name and authority to recommend him, he had become an accepted member of the very select circle of great collectors. To be accepted by these demanding art lovers it was not enough to accumulate masterpieces, he had to display wit, intelligence and above all intuition. His elders called him 'young Schuster', or 'Schusternok'. But these acquaintances and their enlightened advice alone cannot account for the birth of this passion. Another factor was the distinctive flavour of a childhood spent in contact with works which, engraved on his memory, were the seeds from which his entire collection grew.

'My great-grandfather was born in Bykhov in 1828. He came to St Petersburg to supervise the upkeep of the town's many street lamps. He was part of a team whose job was to maintain the

3

Moscow, 1912. German Fyodorov.
Oil on canvas. 100 x 72 cm.

44

town's lighting and, at the end of his career, he was promoted to the rank of a non-commissioned officer and decorated. His portrait was painted in 1901 by Ioffé, who was also a photographer. Marc Chagall worked with him as a photographic retoucher when he was living in St Petersburg. The portrait of my great-grandfather still belongs to the eldest son in our family. I inherited it from my father, and it is the work of Alexander Makovsky, who painted it in 1914. It is a ceremonial portrait in a heavy gilt frame. My grandfather, who died before the Revolution, was a collector. I was born in 1934 and only knew him from the stories my father told me. During the siege of 1941, my family managed to flee the town which was then called Leningrad. My father abandoned everything, except that portrait which he took with him, rolled up with his few belongings. There is no portrait of my father. Times were too hard.' As for Salomon, he posed for his friends, the painters Yuri Vasilyev, Anatoly Zverev and Yuri Zharkhish.

'I am proud of the fact that this "portrait gallery" is so closely linked to St Petersburg, where my family has lived for over a century. In fact, my great-grandfather used to look after those street lamps celebrated by Gogol in *Nevskiy Prospekt*: "But as soon as dusk falls on the streets and on the houses, as soon as the night watchman climbs his ladder to light the street lamps and the prints which no-one dares to display during the day appear in the lower windows of the shops, Nevskiy Prospekt comes to life. This is that mysterious hour when the lamps shed a fantastic and alluring light over everything." And my father, who was an architect, devoted his

4

Salomon Schuster in front of the portrait of his grandfather, painted in 1914 by Alexander Makovsky. This is a ceremonial portrait in a heavy gilt frame. During the siege of Leningrad in 1941, the Schuster family managed to flee the city, carrying with them only the canvas of this portrait rolled up with their few belongings.

45

whole life to preserving the harmony of this town whose geometric precision is tempered by the proximity of the sea and by the golden domes reflected in countless canals.' The family tradition of portraits was not the only one to arouse the collector's precocious interest. 'I was three or four years old,' relates Salomon Schuster, 'and my parents had hung some painted eggs above my little bed to celebrate Easter. I reached out my hands for those fragile trinkets, made of opaline, and red and yellow glass, when my mother told me not to touch them: "Be careful, they date back to the time of Tsar Alexander I and of Pushkin!" These names remained imprinted on my memory. I was to come across Tsar Alexander I again in my history books. But I already knew who Pushkin was. His tales, *The Golden Cockerel* and *Rusalka*, had been read to me. The portrait of him in his youth, an engraving by Geltsman, used to hang in my room.' Pushkin continued to haunt Salomon Schuster, who worshipped 'the inventor' of the modern Russian language, the poet who ennobled the folklore of his country. Salomon Schuster enjoys pointing out their physical similarities: like Pushkin, the descendant

of Ibrahim Hannibal, 'Peter the Great's Negro', he has frizzy hair. He favours the familiar poses of his idol, his head resting on his fist in pensive mode, and he has studied the writer's portraits very closely. He is so obsessive about this identification that his family have nicknamed him 'Pushkinson'.

In the child's imagination, the figure of Pushkin, who drew his inspiration from the legends of ancient Russia, was associated with the glowing colours of Easter eggs, reminiscent of the priceless marvels created by Fabergé for the Tsars. This association must have influenced the future collector's penchant for Russian works with an occasional oriental touch. A dream, emerging from a place more distant than the Steppe, is woven like a golden thread through the history of Russia. Those fabulous eggs, in the child's eyes, were as precious as the gems in *The Arabian Nights*. Many years later, this same influence was evident in his selection of certain artists whose work restored a continuity which had been lost in the vogue for the West: a still life by Mashkov, a landscape by Saryan and a female musician by Pirosmani.

5   6

Sketch of a costume for 'Famira-Kifared'
in the play by I. Annensky, 1916. Alexandra Ekster.
Watercolour on paper. 44.5 x 41 cm.

The Dance, *1917.*
Ignati Nivinsky.
Oil on canvas. 110 x 75 cm.

46

The first stars in this constellation: family portraits, the portrait of Pushkin must be seen in conjunction with a work, linking his childhood memories to his adulthood. In his room, above his bed, hung a drawing by Valentin Serov, entitled *The Botkin Children*. One day, when he was a teenager and half-asleep, he overheard a conversation between his mother and a friend, the sculptor Vladimir Ingal. His mother asked the artist if he thought that the drawing was an original or not. The next day, the young boy was a source of great amusement to his family when he asked them what an 'original' was. Several years later, in 1951, he joined the Film Institute to train as a film director. To his great surprise, he was to meet the 'original' of one of the *Botkin Children*. 'My professor was Lev Vladimirovich Kuleshov, a renowned film-maker from the silent movie era. His wife, Alexandra Sergeevna Khokhlova, worked as his assistant. She was very thin, with red hair and stockings which spiralled down her bony legs. She never went anywhere without an enormous bag crammed with books. She seemed to me to be "an extremely colourful ogress". I told one of my friends, who said that she was one of Tretyakov's granddaughters and therefore the eldest of the

Botkin Children whom Serov had immortalized.' Salomon Schuster remembers having seen the films in which the actress was supremely capable of capitalizing on her unattractive physique. *The Extraordinary Adventures of Mr West in the country of the Bolsheviks* told the story of an American senator's visit to soviet Russia. Khokhlova played the role of an absurd aristocrat who was contriving to show the Yankee how bad the Revolution had been for the country. This parody, which was released in 1924, was greeted enthusiastically by the press. However, the second of the actress's major roles, in *According to the law*, in 1926, was not a success. The film, based on a book by Jack London, conjured up the world of gold miners. Khokhlova was accused of becoming 'Americanized', and her fame dwindled.

'Gradually', says Salomon Schuster, 'the mental picture of the portrait which adorned my room as a child, came to life. The lanky frame of my teacher, the extravagant actress of post-revolutionary cinema, became superimposed on those features which I had known so well for so long. Serov's model had acquired undreamed-of depths. Later, I saw another likeness of Khokhlova at the house of Marianna Lentulov, the painter's

49

7   8

Portrait of an unknown woman, *1917.*
Boris Grigoryev. Oil on Canvas. 95 x 79 cm.

Yevgenia Valentinovna Kryukova, wife of the collector Salomon A. Schuster, comes from Don-Khazan. Her oriental taste tempers her husband's predilection for cold colours. These complementary tastes make the Schuster–Kryukova collection diverse yet harmonious.

50

9
Portrait of Elisaveta S. Potechina,
first wife of the painter, 1917.
Robert Falk. Oil on canvas. 89 x 78 cm.

10
Portrait of a woman, *1918. Aristarkh Lentulov.*
Oil on canvas. 155 x 137 cm.

daughter. She owned a portrait of the actress, painted by her father. Alexandra Sergeevna was wearing a yellow velvet dress, the same one she wore, in 1919, on the day of her Cinema Institute examination, which she passed with flying colours illustrating her potential as a leading actress. The painting now hangs in the Tretyakov gallery and things have come full circle, the granddaughter is reunited with her maternal grandfather in his museum. I crossed the path of the little girl in Serov's drawing for one last time during a stay in the country in a villa owned by Matveesky and exclusively for the use of "veterans" of the cinema. I was in the middle of writing a film scenario, and I was working by the open window when I saw a woman coming up the path. She was walking with a spring in her step, and her eyes, now blind, were raised skywards. I recognized Khokhlova immediately by her inimitable gait and the colour of her hair, which was still flaming red. She passed under my window several times. I wondered how old she could possibly be and tried to work it out in my head, the portrait by Serov dated from 1900 and Alexandra Sergeevna was the eldest. Dusk had gradually enveloped the garden and this tall, thin woman carried on fluttering up and down the path like an injured bird. Eventually, she turned a corner of the house and disappeared forever. She died in 1985, at the age of eighty-eight.

'I was fascinated by this intrusion of reality into the world of art. Like all collectors, I occasionally dream of playing a part in the life of the painters whose work I admire. I have a weakness for portraits which depict people from the artistic world. Looking at them, I get the feeling that I am grasping the mystery of their creation. I admire the pencil sketches of Ehrenburg by Shklovsky, not only because of their aesthetic quality but more because they enable me to break into the world of painters and their models.'

Crossing the room in which the vestiges of his father's collection grace the walls, you come to a sitting-room. Your attention is immediately drawn to a portrait of a man whose commanding presence dominates the room. Salomon Schuster admits that he has never altered the position of this portrait which seems to be a focal point for all the other canvases. Unlike certain collectors, he usually has no objection to moving his canvases and his objects. Neither the painter nor the model, however, are well-known artists. The portrait, by Jacques Chapiro, is of the composer Arthur Lourie, who was born in St Petersburg in 1892 and emigrated to the United States in the twenties, having been director of the music department of the People's Commissariat for Education. But, examining this work more closely, you can see that there is a lack of harmony between the colours, which are very pale and virtually translucent, and the drawing, which is very sharply delineated. It is at the very heart of this contradiction that the dialogue between model and spectator takes place. The painter, therefore, does nothing more than set the scene for this encounter. The

11
Miskhor (Crimean landscape), *1925.*
Pavel Kuznetsov.
Oil on canvas. 72 x 85 cm.

52

transparency of the colours seems to expose the musician's soul, while the keen incisiveness of the drawing makes us feel that the sitter's enquiring gaze is turned on us. You realize that Salomon Schuster, who makes no bones about his fascination for portraits, has made this painting the unavowed centre of his collection. Chapiro's canvas exerts the ambiguous charm of any portrait; it is simultaneously an enigma for us to puzzle over and a straightforward statement of our domestic life. Schuster's search for portraits plays an important part in the creation of his collection: 'The first time I visited the studio of the Armenian painter, Saryan, to whom I had been introduced by Pavel Kuznetsov, I saw two portraits which I immediately coveted, one of the composer Shostakovich, and the other of the poet Anna Akhmatova. Saryan didn't want to sell them to me, and even though he had some magnificent canvases there from his early period, I didn't buy anything. I only had eyes for those portraits.'

The name of Anna Akhmatova, like the name of Pushkin before, is linked to Salomon Schuster's personal history. On 5 March 1966, one of the greatest voices in Russian poetry was silenced in Moscow. Akhmatova was buried a few days later in Komarovo, near Leningrad. Salomon Schuster took his camera and went to film the funeral of the woman who, in everyone's eyes, had come to be the embodiment of resistance to tyranny. The authorities never did succeed in breaking the courage shown by

Anna Akhmatova, who took her pseudonym from the name of the last Tartar Khans who struck fear into the hearts of the people of Moscow. She continued to produce her admirable work in the face of harassment and the worst acts of cruelty, of her first husband being sentenced to death, of her only son being deported to Siberia and of her own imprisonment in Leningrad. She said in 1940: 'When you are standing in a queue, in the sleet, to buy some red herring, assailed by an odour which will cling to your shoes and your coat for another ten days and suddenly, behind you, someone begins to murmur your lines, that really means something'. Reciting banned poems or collecting works of art was, in Soviet Russia, a form of resistance.

'It was in March 1966,' relates Salomon Schuster, 'I was working at Lenfilm but I had kept in touch with my friends at the Documentary Studio in Leningrad. It was with them that I decided to organize the coverage of Anna Akhmatova's funeral. I obtained the permission of her daughter-in-law and the agreement of the Union of Writers. Don't forget that in 1966 we were right in the middle of the "period of stagnation", as it is called now. All the media were under close surveillance. Solovtsev, the director of the Leningrad Documentary Studio agreed to give us two hundred metres of film and, after lengthy discussions, we were able to extract an additional four hundred metres and a camera which could make sound recordings. We took the opportunity to obtain

12
Kirghiz family, *1910*.
Pavel Kuznetsov.
Oil on canvas. 67.5 x 76 cm.

53

permission to film in the church. We had to phone the Soviet Executive Committee of the town, who advised us to inform the Party's Regional Committee. But we did not do that.

People were up in arms about our intrusion in the church. Akhmatova's son was furious. I tried to convince him that this documentary was a testimony to the passionate response that his mother's poetry evoked everywhere. But as soon as we began to shoot the film, someone rushed up and shouted that we were under orders to return to the Studio immediately. I hid myself a little farther off and continued to film the procession. Later, my friend, Aranovich, explained that the Party's Regional Committee, which had got wind of our project, had prohibited filming inside the church. The Studio was plunged into panic, all the entrances and exits were monitored. Unfortunately, we had already sent the cassettes of the sound recording to the Studio. They were confiscated and were never heard of again.

Leaving the Cathedral of St Nicholas, the funeral procession crossed the Kirov Bridge and headed towards the Sheremetev Palace, the 'House of Fountains' where Anna Akhmatova lived in a wretched room in a communal apartment. Finally we arrived at Lenin Street where she lived at the end of her life. Then we left town, because the writer was to be buried in Komarovo, where she used to spend her childhood holidays; a spot that she liked to revisit.

The very next day, we learned the price we would have to pay. Aranovich was demoted to the level of assistant for three months even though he was a director. I was no longer invited to the Documentary Studio or offered work there. This lasted for twenty-three years. It took me a month to find out the reason for this disgrace: the Party had not liked the fact that we had filmed in the church, as we were civil servants working for the State. But they did promise me that they would not destroy the document. In

55

13
Apple blossom, *1909.*
Natalya Goncharova.
Oil on canvas. 92 x 103 cm.

14
Red earth, *1909.*
David Burlyuk.
Oil on canvas. 70 x 130 cm.

fact, twenty years later, the director Dyakonov was to use some of our shots for his film *The Temple* and Aranovich made a film about Akhmatova which used our footage.'

In 1958, several years before filming Anna Akhmatova's funeral, Salomon Schuster learnt that the regime had just blacklisted Boris Pasternak and forced him to refuse the Nobel Prize which he had just been awarded. The collector bought six drawings of Leonid Pasternak, the poet's father from one of his friends and sent them to the poet, by way of a homage.

'Collecting is the only opportunity we have to exercise choice in a society which tends to standardize everything. This is the only way we can assert our independence.' If you cannot run your own life, whose circumscribed limits are laid down by over-zealous authorities, you can at least choose the works of art which you wish to live with. For that, you need a tenacious streak which is, in his view, the hallmark of any true collector. Such tenacity is occasionally miraculously rewarded, as this anecdote, also linked to a portrait, shows. 'During the fifties, I made the acquaintance of

15
Still life with fruit, *1908.*
Ilya Mashkov.
Oil on canvas. 104 x 132 cm.

a Muscovite book-lover, Nikolai Pavlovich Smirnov-Sokolsky. We became great friends, so much so that we wanted to make a film together, a project that was never realized. Smirnov-Sokolsky collected books and drawings, in particular those concerning Pushkin. Like me, only worse, he was afflicted by Pushkinmania. However, among the relics of his favourite poet, was a work which made you wonder why it was there. It was the portrait of a young man sitting on a window-sill, set against the background of a brightly coloured landscape. He was wearing an arrogant

expression and was swinging his foot towards the foreground of the painting so that his shoe took up as much space as his face did. I asked Smirnov-Sokolsky why he exhibited that canvas, which I felt did not fit the "profile" of his collection. I had recognized the portrait of Vasily Shukhaev by his friend Alexander Yakovlev, whose sketches I had seen at the home of Yakovlev's ex-wife, the actress [Kasarosa]. This group of artists was the talk of the town in St Petersburg before the revolution but went their different ways in the twenties. Yakovlev emigrated to France, then to the United

16
Nude models in the studio, *1916.*
Ilya Mashkov.
Oil on canvas. 147 x 156 cm.

57

States, while Shukhaev, after several years in exile, returned to Russia, where he was almost immediately arrested and deported to Magadan. Insist as I might, Smirnov-Sokolsky refused to let me have the portrait of "Vaska Shukhaev by Sachka Yakovlev". I realized from the affectionate diminutives he was using that he had known the painter and his model extremely well and that it was no accident that the painting was in a collection devoted to the age of Pushkin. But I offered him an exchange, as we often did as collectors. I would look for some almanacs from Pushkin's era, and when I had spent the three thousand rubles which the painting cost, he would give it to me. For several years I bought almanacs and would take them one after the other to Nikolai Pavlovich. He would accept them and thank me, but didn't say another word on the subject. Finally, I reminded him of his promise, and that it was time for him to give me the portrait of Vaska Shukhaev. He asked me to bring him one more almanac and the painting would be mine. Smirnov-Sokolsky died soon after and I didn't have the heart to remind his widow about the exchange agreement we had entered into. The valuable books were given to the Lenin library, but I don't know what became of the painting. At the beginning of the eighties, I learned of the death of the collector's widow. For the first time in twenty years, my thoughts turned again to the portrait. Several years later, I was in Moscow to introduce one of my films, *Lights,* adapted from a short story by Chekhov. Shortly before my trip, I had mentioned in passing to my wife how much I regretted losing track of Yakovlev's painting. "Don't worry", she replied, "if that painting is destined to be part of our collection, it will be, one way or another." And on 29 December 1984, having screened my film at the Goskino, I decided to buy myself a present. I went into an antique shop on the Smolensky Quay. At first, I didn't see anything of interest. But I always follow my father's advice: "Never be in a hurry. Remember that a collector is a museum in himself. He is its most reliable expert and its most knowledgeable official". And suddenly, I glimpsed, half-hidden behind a pillar, a framed canvas: the portrait of Vaska Shukhaev by Yakovlev. I bought it immediately. The shop assistant smiled sceptically at my enthusiasm. She told me that the work had been there for four months, that the experts at the Tretyakov Gallery had seen it and considered it to be of no interest. In fact, there was a label attached to it: "08.09.84. Expert's report from the Tretyakov Gallery. Portrait of an unknown man by an unknown painter". The antique shop owner had already been forced to lower his price. And indeed, the signature on the painting had become illegible, but it was signed for all that. The model's foot, casually swung across the canvas is in itself tantamount to a signature. It is unmistakeable to the true connoisseur.' On the other hand, a signature can be meaningless, as one of the great collectors of the forties and fifties, Boris N. Okunev, used to say: 'Despite the signature, it's a fake'.

The doyen of the circle of collectors to which 'Schusternok' had gained admittance at the age of seventeen, was Grigory Samuilovich Blok, a lawyer. He taught the young man that art lovers fall into two categories: those who use their ears and those who trust their eyes. Only the latter belonged to the true breed of collectors.

Blok advised him always to follow his instincts: 'You must buy the works you like even if you don't know the name of the artist, and trust your intuition.' 'Among the discoveries that I made by following this advice', relates Salomon Schuster, 'was a French canvas. Ten years ago, I met some people who still owned what remained of a collection put together by their grandfather. I was shown several paintings I didn't like. But I spotted a work that interested me immediately. A watercolour on board, which depicted a group of Breton peasants around a table. My hosts were certain that this painting was by Grigoryev. This painter was made fashionable in the twenties by the publisher, Burtsev, whose collection was broken up after he was sentenced to deportation. The people I was speaking to owned several pieces from the Burtsev collection, which accounts for their mistake. Looking at the group of Bretons, I couldn't help thinking of Gauguin, then Van Gogh. Finally, I remembered the school of Pont Aven. After that rapid analysis, I set about persuading my hosts to sell me the painting. They took some coaxing because the lady of the house was particularly fond of that canvas. I kept quiet about my supposed attribution to avoid pushing up the price. I managed to buy this work, which I examined at length at home. I found a catalogue of the Pont Aven painters and I considered my purchase from every angle. Suddenly, I succeeded in making out the signature, which was virtually illegible: Louis Roy. The name of the painter appeared in my catalogue. He was a very interesting and rare artist. No Russian museum owns a work by him, but it is one of the discoveries that I am most proud of.'

There is some justification for including apparently second-rate works in a collection. They can say much about the way in which the artistic collection has been put together. To see a collection merely as a systematic accumulation of masterpieces would be absurd. Salomon Schuster cites, with regard to artistic 'errors', the anecdote about Delacroix and Antoine Louis Barye. The latter, a famous painter of animals, pointed out to Delacroix that he had painted the profile of a horse with one eye as viewed from the front. Delacroix handed him his palette and brush and asked him to correct this fault, which apparently made the animal look implausible. Barye did so, then stood back to assess the effect he had produced. After a brief silence, he went back to the easel and repainted the profile of the head with the eye seen from straight on, as Delacroix had done, and apologized.

The same holds true for a collection whose mediocre works are inextricably bound to its exceptional pieces, and what seems like an error often reveals the secret of its originality. The collector may prefer a picture which endorses his unerring eye, like the watercolour by Louis Roy for Salomon Schuster, to a universally acclaimed masterpiece. The only thing that matters is the affinity, 'the emotional sympathy', to use Salomon Schuster's expression, which binds a work to its owner, and which links the works to each other. This is because a collection is simultaneously an independent organism and a reflection of the life of the person who has gradually built it up. What Salomon Schuster likes best are cold colours, and blue is the chromatic leitmotif running through his collection, starting with the blue and white Chinese vase bought at the age of twelve. This piece of porcelain was the beginning of the fabulous collection, so much admired now. Its oriental colouring is bathed in the light of St Petersburg, a town in which Salomon Schuster has lived all his life. In his novel *Petersburg*, Andrey Bely conjures up the 'bluish expanses on the far side of the Neva' and 'the turquoise of an icy sky' against which towers 'the sparkling dome of St Isaac'.

The collector's personal history, his attachment to St Petersburg, combined with the actual inclusion of certain works gives his collection its distinctive identity. Boris Grigoryev's portrait

58

17
Province of Gourzouff (Solntsedar), *1913.*
Aristarkh Lentulov.
Oil on canvas. 87 x 95.5 cm.

of a woman could, by itself, symbolize this taste for icy transparency. The hard brilliance of the colours transforms the model into a porcelain figurine. And, despite the several vivid touches in the background of the painting, the scene is devoted to the nocturnal magic of blue.

His love of blue is linked to his fondness of the Orient, which has its roots in Salomon Schuster's childhood. The canvases by Pavel Kuznetsov, one of his favourite painters, are a clear indication of this. *Sheep Shearing* picks up the celestial shades of the mosaics at Bukhara and Samarkand. From his trips to central Asia, in 1910–1911, Kuznetsov brought back various works whose chromatic subtlety was inspired by Persian miniatures.

Martiros Sergeevich Saryan was an Armenian who also drew his inspiration from oriental sources. Salomon Schuster owns a wonderful blue and gold landscape by him which transforms a mountain scene into a fairy-tale setting. This fondness for the Orient owes a great deal to the personality of Salomon Schuster's wife, Yevgeniya Valentinovna Kryukova, who is from Don-Khazan. The collector gives her full credit and admits that her tastes often differ from his. Yevgeniya Kryukova prefers warm colours that remind her of her native country. It is probably due to her influence that the collection includes the superb *Still life with fruit* by Ilya Mashkov. A sumptuous setting of fabric and fruit is spread out around the tall Persian vase. Miraculously, and herein lies the

60

18
Still life with lily and fan, *1918.*
Alexander Osmyorkin.
Oil on canvas. 69 x 55 cm.

19
Abstraction, *1921.*
Antonina Sofronova.
Oil on canvas. 47 x 40 cm.

20

Orchestrated self-portrait. *Kirill Zdanevich. Watercolour on card. 76 x 153 cm.*
FROM LEFT TO RIGHT *Lado Gudiashvili (painter in the twenties and thirties),*
Kara-Dervish (Armenian futurist poet), Kirill Zdanevich (painter),
Ilya Zdanevich (poet, founder of the '41' group) and Alexei Kruchyonykh (futurist poet and engraver).

mysterious charm of the work, the assortment of ornamental motifs possesses an unusual harmony. The apparent disorder of the materials with their warm colours revolves around the green and white china whose architectural role is accentuated by the fluid green painting which gives the decorative flat colours an unexpected depth. The warm colours create a spectacular effect; while the chilly greens and whites bring out the discreet, precise structure. Schuster tells an anecdote about this canvas which illustrates how people could, not so long ago, build up a collection in the former USSR: 'One day, going into a bakery, imagine my surprise when I saw a superb still life by Mashkov in the back of the shop. I asked how the masterpiece had come to be there and the baker replied that a bankrupt millionaire had bartered the painting for bread. I immediately asked to buy the canvas, but the baker who refused point blank explained: 'We use the painting to hide a stain which spoils the appearance of the wall in that room. We haven't got any paint to redecorate it so we leave that painting there.' I immediately offered to pay for the back of the shop to be redecorated in exchange for Mashkov's still life and the baker and his wife accepted enthusiastically. I can still see myself carrying the

21
Portrait of the composer Arthur Lourie, *1923.*
Jacques Chapiro. Mixed media on board. 53 x 44 cm.

painting to my car, showered by blessings from the two elderly proprietors.'

Looking at the painting by Mashkov, you can see how the talents of these two collectors, Salomon Schuster and Yevgeniya Kryukova, complement each other. Other still lifes, those by Shterenberg or Falk, are more abstract. They belong to the 'cold' side of the collection, which, despite everything, dominates the warmer colour tones. Two of the finest pieces in the collection are by Niko Pirosmani. This Georgian painter, who lived from 1863 to 1918, is called 'the Russian Douanier Rousseau'. Salomon Schuster

owns two portraits by this 'naive' artist who was self-taught and inspired by the popular traditions of Georgia. The portrait of the female musician (*Georgina playing the tambourine*) is executed on oilcloth. Pirosmani actually used very mixed media and was more at home, unlike most of the 'naive' painters, with large formats. The huge silhouette of Georgina is sketched in white paint but meticulous attention is paid to her plump face, her lace and her tambourine. Every aspect of this figure exudes a joyful vitality and the golden bird on the musician's breast symbolizes the purity of the people's soul. The second portrait by Pirosmani is that of a

21
Portrait of the painter Fabri, *1911.*
Robert Falk. Oil on canvas. 112 x 86 cm.

65

painter, I. Zdanevich, who helped him make a name for himself among Russian artists. The model is posing in a forest clearing as if he were in a studio, but the artificiality and touching awkwardness of his pose are given warmth by rich ochre and brown monochrome, clearly illustrating the painter's considerable talent. Salomon Schuster's family knew Zdanevich's, so that once again personal history is inextricably linked to the works of art.

Pirosmani was also responsible for a transaction between Salomon Schuster and the famous collector, Kostakis. The latter parted with one of the canvases in exchange for a Kandinsky which Salomon Schuster owned. This way of going about things is typical of Russian collectors: their method of building up a collection mirrors the unofficial economy of the country. They share the various artistic *oeuvres* between them, which means Kostakis had priority rights on works by Malevich, Chagall and Kandinsky, or else they buy pieces which are not particularly to their taste, intending to exchange them with another collector. Salomon

Schuster bought some Japanese etchings for this purpose, but when the collector with whom he was exchanging the engravings died, he developed a passion for Japan in his own right. The collections are essential to each other's existence and the resonance between them is similar to that which links the works within a single collection. But, beneath the surface of any collection worthy of that name, the personality of its owner can be glimpsed. Collecting works produces an autobiography, partially imaginary, of the collector. Each work is a mirror in which the collector sees his own reflection. The canvas by Drevin, in whose paintings reality dissolves in a white haze peopled with ghostly figures, does this for Salomon Schuster: 'Very early in the morning, I like to watch the sun's rays moving towards Drevin's canvas, which depicts a boat, a sail. When the sunshine finally strikes the painting, I see a face where the sail should be. This reminds me of my childhood, the glass Easter eggs, and I think I see a smile on the face of the little girl in Serov's portrait, constantly there yet lost forever.'

23
Still life with yellow cup, *1920.*
David Shterenberg.
Oil on canvas. 70 x 50 cm.

24
Still life with pomegranates, *circa 1910–20.*
David Shterenberg.
Oil on canvas. 63 x 52 cm. Oval.

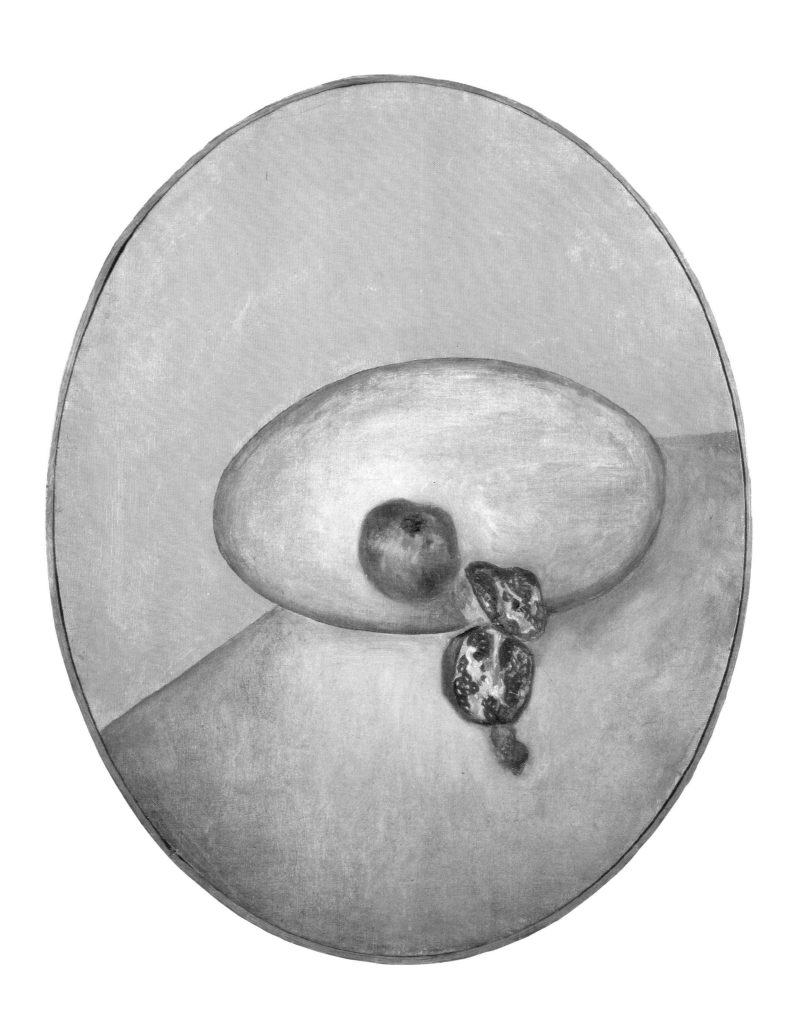

25

Breaking with family tradition, Salomon Schuster prefers contemporary Russian painting to the canvases by seventeenth- and eighteenth-century western European masters which made up the majority of his father's collection.

26

Portrait of Salomon A. Schuster. *Anatoly Zverev. Watercolour on paper. Around 60 x 40 cm.*

68

27
Peace, celebration, liberation, *1917. Aristarkh Lentulov.*
On the back, portrait of 1918. Oil on canvas. 155 x 137 cm.

VALENTINA GOLOD'S COLLECTION

1 - 2

Valentina Golod, granddaughter of one of Tsarina Maria Fyodorovna's ladies-in-waiting, has recreated, with an impeccable use of colour, the hushed, sophisticated atmosphere of the homes of the aristocracy in St Petersburg. In the bedroom, a vivid red provides a setting for the fine collection of malachite objects, one of Valentina Golod's passions.

There is an enclave, deep in a sinister courtyard in the heart of St Petersburg that time has left untouched. Behind a heavy baize-covered door, the golden sheen of bronzes and mirrors softens the chilly light of the city. This is the home of Valentina Mikhailovna Golod but it could be the palace of a Russian prince at the beginning of the nineteenth century. The suite of rooms, each papered in a different colour, forms a backdrop for a collection of paintings and objects which rekindle the splendour of the past. Many of them belonged to Valentina M. Golod's parents. Her father, who was a lawyer in St Petersburg and a major landowner, married to the daughter of the famous General Kotlyarevsky, whom Pushkin nicknamed in a poem 'the scourge of the Caucasus', was one of the first targets when the Revolution broke out. Valentina, born in 1905, was twelve years old when she saw the dead body of her mother lying in front of the entrance to one of her family's properties, assassinated by the Reds. The revolutionaries broke into the house where the little girl was alone with her younger sister

and her French governess. The latter was in bed, suffering from typhus fever. One of the officers, catching sight of a piano, ventured to pick out several chords. Valentina Golod needed no encouragement to bang the lid down on his fingers saying: 'Be quiet; Mademoiselle is ill.'

The little girls and their governess were saved by their mother's dressmaker, who arrived to take them to St Petersburg. Here, they were reunited with the girls' grandmother who had been a lady-in-waiting to the Tsarina Maria Fyodorovna, wife of Alexander III. Valentina Golod's father emigrated and his daughter never saw him again. It was not until the seventies that she obtained a visa for France in order to spend a brief summer with her emigrant family.

She was brought up by her grandmother and governess, and received an impeccable education worthy of the famous Smolny Institute founded by Catherine II for young ladies belonging to the nobility. Despite the unsettled times, she was

relatively sheltered by the two women who led a very secluded life among the vestiges of their former luxury. She spoke French without an accent and became a translator of literary works and stage plays. Moving in artistic circles, she spent her leisure time taking courses in applied art and became very skilled in restoring antique objects.

Valentina Golod was not satisfied with merely preserving the vestiges of the family collection. With unerring intuition and surprising tenacity, she breathed new life into these objects by recreating the extravagant atmosphere of Pavlovsk, the small palace given by Catherine II to her son, Paul. The St Petersburg apartment seems like a small-scale reproduction of the imperial residence, which was built at the very end of the eighteenth century on the outskirts of the town and is set in breath-taking landscaped grounds. The same discreet and sophisticated taste governs the way Valentina Golod's rooms are arranged. Each object has been chosen for its opulence, but must also blend in with the harmonious colour scheme, quietly playing its part in creating an overall sense of unity.

Valentina gradually added to the family collection by unearthing treasures in the antique shops of St Petersburg. This painstaking search, an impassioned quest sorting through the bric-a-brac of second-hand shops, is her life's work. She is very reticent about her past. All we know is that she has been married twice and has no children. On the other hand, she cannot say enough about her collection.

'I collected everything I liked, she says, everything that caught my attention. My particular interest in the late eighteenth century and the early nineteenth century dates from 1930. I gradually weeded out all the objects which did not date from this period, achieving complete stylistic unity within my home. Furthermore, I realized things have a mysterious life of their own, attracting each other as if by magnetism, whatever obstacles are put in their way. For example, I owned a little mahogany corner cupboard, it was very rare and seemed destined to remain alone; but not at all, I discovered its counterpart. I restored two mahogany armchairs and finally, years later, I was able to get hold of a matching sofa. This set is a perfect example of an early nineteenth-

3
Portrait of Miss Elena Rayevsky, *1820.*
Anthelme-François Lagrenée. Gouache on ivory. 8 x 6.8 cm.

century drawing-room. On another occasion, as luck would have it, I unearthed a ruby-coloured glass, with bronze decoration. I began to build up a collection of glassware around it, in exactly the same colour and with exactly the same decoration. So what started out as a stroke of luck turned into a matter of personal taste and deliberate choice.'

Valentina Golod's approach to collecting is somewhat similar to that of Morozov. The latter left empty spaces on his walls for paintings that he did not yet own but which one day he was sure would take their place. He treated his collection like a jigsaw puzzle, patiently collecting its pieces one by one. A fragmented whole, put back together again and brought back to life.

What matters to Valentina is not exhibiting her valuable objects, nor using them like props for a showy stage set. She takes pride in giving them a new lease of life, firstly by restoring them with skill and affection and then by including them as a natural part of the intimate surroundings of her daily life. She has boundless affection for very badly damaged objects. She points out a box decorated with miniatures, which takes the theme from La Fontaine's *Fables*, a French curio from the end of the eighteenth century. When she bought it, there were four miniatures missing and no lid. By dint of sheer perseverance, she located some miniatures which could replace the ones that had disappeared. Then, with pieces of agate and small fragments of mother-of-pearl, she designed a lid which a restorer then reconstructed for her. This 'salvaged' object is one of her favourite pieces. It is representative of her collection, which aims to restore past treasures tarnished by the vicissitudes of history to their former glory.

Glassware is more at risk than any other thing of beauty. Its fragility works a particular brand of magic, which can be awakened by a shaft of light or shattered into a thousand pieces by a single touch. Valentina Golod's collection includes some superb examples of the art of glassmaking, which are for the most part, manufactured in Russia. In the rather confined rooms, the variegated light flashing from the pendants and crystals on the chandeliers makes the air quiver. In the display cases and on the tables, brief sparks are given off by vases or the facets of cut glass. There is a surprising variety of shapes but one predominant colour,

4   **5**

Portrait of Varvara Lupukhina, *1835–40. Anonymous.*
Gouache on ivory. 8.5 x 7.2 cm.
This portrait could be the work of the poet and painter,
Lermontov, who was in love with Varvara Lupukhina.

Probably the Portrait of the young prince
Mikhailovich Volkonsky, 1809. Domenico Bossi.

a deep red often chased in gold or combined with bronze. Stoppers decorated by Tamir, delicate pale pink dishes, vases with bases of bronze gryphons are like a set of variations played in a minor key, that relieve the flamboyant red harmonies of the finest pieces in this collection, such as a carafe made of ruby-coloured glass and two flutes dating back to the end of the eighteenth century. On each of the rococo-style flutes two engraved, symmetrical medallions depict respectively a gentleman and a lady playing music, facing each other in a concert. This is reminiscent of a *fête galante*, at Versailles or Pavlovsk, before the revolutionary upheaval. Certain pieces are oddly shaped: a vase in the shape of a pear made of gold-coloured glass decorated with enamel, or a spherical lilac-coloured vase which dates from the first half of the nineteenth century. But your attention is soon caught by the huge number of perfume bottles, one of Valentina Golod's passions. This part of the collection started with the purchase of a bottle in the shape of a bird. This was gradually followed by other examples, to represent the evolution of the genre between the classical period and 'modern art', which is the term used to describe *art nouveau* in Russia. Semi-circular spheres shimmering like bubbles, flat bottles which could be slipped into a bodice, clear crystal or glassware heavy with gold and medallions display the most extravagant diversity. Coloured glass fired the imagination of an entire era between 1750 and 1850. The scientist, Mikhail Lomonosov, founder of the University of Moscow in 1755, researched ways of refining the technique of colouring glass. Gradually, as tastes changed, gold and silver decorations became heavier and heavier until they completely covered and obscured the glass itself. Towards the middle of the nineteenth century, a garish polychromatic finish replaced the delicate shades which characterize bottles from the previous century.

One might wonder whether Valentina Golod's liking for tiny objects stems from the day her grandmother gave her a miniature compass case made of gold and agate. Indeed, this

74

6

In the drawing-room, rows of intricately-worked miniatures hang beneath the portrait of the Grand Duchess, Elena Pavlovna, the beloved aunt of Tsar Alexander II. This work determines the room's décor. The blue walls pick up the colours in Elena Pavlovna's dress and the mahogany of the early nineteenth-century furniture accentuates the tawny colour of the leather bindings she is holding in her hands.

apartment, which is jealously guarded from the world outside, contains an impressive profusion of intricately-worked trinkets, restored and cared for with the meticulous attention and patience of a miniaturist from years gone by. 'The miniature is a narrow door that opens on to a whole new world.' (Gaston Bachelard). This is probably the secret behind Valentina Golod's unusual collection. Wrapped in the infinite detail of such minute objects, she has been able to elude the despair of day-to-day existence. The mother-of-pearl marquetry of a box which fits in the palm of your hand or the enchanting menagerie of animals made of semi-precious stones all go to make up this 'miniature world', to use Bachelard's phrase. A world which turns our view of reality upside down and creates a 'mini' universe in our imagination.

The mysteriousness of things is in inverse proportion to their size. One day, Valentina Golod noticed that one of her most beautiful miniatures, depicting the Empress Alexandra Fyodorovna, wife of Nicholas I, was covered in dust, inside its protective glass cover. The portrait was painted on ivory, which meant that it was very fragile. After some hesitation, she decided to clean it and removed the miniature from its wide velvet surround. Imagine her surprise when she discovered a small gold box, under the surround! It contained a tiny lock of hair and a playing card the size of a thumb-nail, a nine of hearts, a symbol of love. To whom had the Empress given her portrait and this token of passion? Such a beautiful woman, extolled by Pushkin, would have been duty bound to keep her feelings under lock and key. But she entrusted the intimate riddle of her heart to the miniature, that might have been intended for the dashing A. V. Trubetskoy, a horseman in the Imperial Guard, for whom, it was rumoured, she had a special fondness. Other portraits, on snuff-boxes made of tortoiseshell or ivory, call to mind familiar figures. Charlotte Corday, whose portrait was painted by the French painter H. Lapis, looks passionate, with an exultant expression and mobile features. Another snuff-box shows the sister of Tsar Alexander I, the Grand

7
Portrait of Yekaterina Rayevsky, *wife of Count Orlov,*
around 1820. Anthelme-François Lagrenée.
Gouache on ivory. 8.7 x 8.7 cm.

8 - 9

In the boudoir adjoining the bedroom, the walls papered in green draw their warmth from the crimson and ruby accents of the sofa and the curtains. Everywhere in these narrow rooms mirrors create the impression of space, opening up trompe-l'oeil *vistas. Everywhere, light refracted by the crystal of the chandeliers compensates for the chilly daylight outside, against which the curtains usually remain closed.*

Duchess, Yekaterina Pavlovna, wearing a formal gown and diadem. She was a fierce patriot, refused to marry Napoleon I and transformed her Tver residence into the headquarters of the anti-French resistance movement. Her sister, Maria Pavlovna, is depicted on a third snuff-box. She lived in Weimar, where she reigned at the side of her husband, Duke Karl Friedrich. Goethe, who knew her, described her as follows: 'She is intelligent, kind-hearted and benevolent. She is a great asset to our country.' Later, he added: 'The duchess is one of the most remarkable women of our times. Her rank doesn't change a thing. The most important quality for a sovereign to have is a personality which remains unaffected by the decorum surrounding it.'

The finest part of the Golod collection is the miniatures, a true mini-museum which features the names of the best painters of the genre: Anthelme-François Lagrenée, Domenico Bossi, Pietro Rossi, Jean-Baptiste Singry. In 1970, there was an exhibition in the Pushkin House, on the Moika in Leningrad, where the public was struck by the beauty of the miniatures lent by Valentina Golod. The portrait which received the most attention was that of Elena Rayevsky, painted in Gourzouff, in the Crimea, during the summer of 1820. Pushkin was staying with the Rayevsky family at the time, which accounts for the miniature's inclusion in the exhibition. Anthelme Lagrenée, who lived in Russia between 1817 and 1825, having already made his name in Europe, had painted the portrait and, during the same period, had painted a medallion depicting Elena's sister, Yekaterina, who was to become the wife of Count Orlov. Despite the confined area he was working in, Lagrenée was able to place his models in appropriate settings giving the attentive observer clues to the personality of both sisters. He placed the romantic Yekaterina in front of a Tartar village, surrounded by cypress trees and the delicate Elena against a mountain landscape. The first exudes the exotic charm of an oriental-style setting, the second is an evocation of ancient Germanic legends, peopled with elves and sylphs. Elena, suffering from tuberculosis, seems doomed to live only as long as the fleeting springtime enjoyed by the roses which crown her melancholy face with its blue eyes. Valentina Golod also possesses other miniatures of the Rayevsky family, that of the youngest daughter, Sofia, and of their mother, Maria.

Another of the marvels in her collection is the work of Jean-Baptiste Singry, Isabey's pupil. This is the portrait of the singer E. P. Lunina, wearing a red dress with white feathers, trimmed with shimmering pearls. The young woman was thirty-five when Singry painted her, at the height of her legendary beauty. In 1820, she married an Italian singer, Count Ricci, whose portrait, painted by the same artist, can be found in the Pushkin Museum. The darling of the most select social circles of the time, E. P. Lunina, whose brother was involved in the Decembrists' uprising along with Pushkin, had only a brief taste of fame before ending her life in poverty. Once she had left her husband, she lived in extremely straitened circumstances. She treasured the letter in which Pushkin paid homage to her artistic talents, a souvenir of the times when she would hold the guests of Princess Zinaida Volkonskaya spellbound. The princess was, in the words of a contemporary, 'a fairy godmother to music'; in her salon, 'everything sang; thoughts, feelings, conversation, movements – everything revolved around music'. A simple miniature evokes all the refinement and passion of a past which is almost, but not quite, tangible.

Is the unknown woman in Borovikovsky's portrait A. P. Kozlyaninovna, the young woman with a pointed chin and full lips in the museum in Pskov, to whom she bears a strange resemblance? Or is she N. I. Lvov, wife of the composer, F. P. Lvov? If you take the trouble to examine the miniature with a magnifying glass you will discover that the first supposition is correct. You can then see that the model is wearing a cameo of Empress Catherine II in profile. When A. P. Kozlyaninovna, who was a gifted painter and sculptor, visited Catherine at Pskov, she gave her two wax figures she had made. Was the cameo given to her by way of thanks? It is very possible. The resemblance between the young girl from Pskov and the wife of the composer Lvov, could be explained by the distant kinship between the two families. If you want to get to the bottom of the secret world of miniatures, you must lose yourself, magnifying glass in hand, in their tiny and intricate mazes. These miniatures, and many others, are arranged in rows under a splendid portrait of the Grand Duchess, Yelena Pavlovna, a canvas of normal size. Valentina Golod particularly likes this painting, which has been made famous by many reproductions. Without a shadow of a doubt it is the work of Christina Robertson, and was probably painted during one of the Grand Duchess's trips to Paris in the first half of the nineteenth century.

The artist and her model had a lot in common. They were both German by birth and Parisian by choice. This likemindedness can be observed in the portrait, which focuses on the inordinate elegance and utter simplicity of Yelena Pavlovna, about whom Valentina Golod talks with great enthusiasm. The Grand Duchess was a great influence on the reformist policies of her nephew, Tsar Alexander II, who abolished serfdom in Russia in 1861. 'She was a highly intelligent woman with a heart of gold', Kiselev said of her. 'She knew how to surround herself with a magnificent court and gave delightful soirées and dinner parties. Her guests were not invited because of their social status, but because of the personal qualities displayed by each individual [...]. Her liberal behaviour caused an uproar amongst the aristocracy.' Neshchersky wrote that 'her kind-heartedness and her intelligence have earned the Grand Duchess Elena Pavlovna the right to rank alongside the great names in Russian history.' In the painting owned by Valentina Golod, the Grand Duchess is still young and turns to look at us. She is at home in this apartment, surrounded by a style of decor that is similar to the one in which she lived. Some of these objects could have belonged to her: for example, this desk set made of malachite, one of Valentina Golod's favourite materials. All the objects in it, – paper-weight, clock, paper holder, box and candelabra – were manufactured by the Peterhof Imperial factory. Their understated refinement, typical of the style in the 1830s, echoes the discreet elegance of the Grand Duchess's portrait where she is simply surrounded by books and flowers. The malachite set is one of the rarities in the Golod collection. On the dressing-table in the bedroom, the lid of one box is decorated with a miniature portrait of Prince Pyotr Mikhailovich Volkonsky, the owner of the house on the Moika where Pushkin lived shortly before his death. With consummate skill, the craftsmen have decorated the chest with *putti* and garlands of bronze roses, and they have designed a small mirror which reflects the prince's face. On the lid of another box, near to the dressing-table set, there is a bronze medal depicting the Smolny Convent, the boarding school for young ladies of the aristocracy. It bears this inscription: '1847–1928, in memory of the Empress Maria Fyodorovna'. In the shadows, the green shimmer of malachite creates the illusion of a luxurious lifestyle which is now unheard of, but which, thanks to Valentina Golod, has been preserved.

VLADIMIR I. PALEEV'S COLLECTION

The collection once owned by Professor Ilya Isaakovich Paleev, who died several years ago, now belongs to his son, Vladimir Ilich, who was born in 1935. Since the collector's death, nothing has been altered in the apartment, which is situated within the Science Academy in St Petersburg, on the quay Peter the Great. The paintings still hang in the same place, covered by thick glass to protect them from the toxic fumes of the city's heating system, whose installations are within the precincts of the Academy.

Professor Ilya I. Paleev was a physicist and occupied the chair of Thermodynamics at the University of Leningrad until his death. He began his collection immediately after the war, in 1948–9, by purchasing a work by Vladimir Lebedev *(The Mincer)*. This initial choice was very revealing in terms of the academic's deep-rooted predilections. It showed that art, for him, was not a means of escapism but gave him access to a more tangible world from which he was too often alienated by his scientific research. Ilya Paleev did not appreciate non-figurative painting. His collection could be summed up by David Burlyuk, one of his favourite artists, describing Monet's *Rouen Cathedral*: 'There, close up, under the glass, some moss was growing, delicately painted in shades of orange, lilac, yellow. Looking at these coloured fibrillae, you would have said, (and it was true enough) that the colour had roots'.

Each of the canvases chosen by I. Paleev is deeply rooted in reality. In order to paint *The Mincer*, Vladimir Lebedev had to exercise the precision of a geometrician and the sensitivity of a musician. The sense of rhythm he brought into play when he orchestrated his still lifes, the one 'with mandolin' for example, confers a huge amount of dignity on even the smallest object. His series of female nudes, several superb examples of which are included in Paleev's collection, are depicted in black ink, barely softened by grey, portraying the sensuous curves of their flesh with a disturbingly life-like result. Although he dropped the idea of collecting works by Malevich or Kandinsky, he unearthed paintings by artists who were part of the national tradition: Pavel Kuznetsov who was representative of the early twentieth century, Boris Grigoryev and, in particular, Kuzma Petrov-Vodkin. Behind Ilya Paleev's enthusiasm for these artists, who were re-establishing Russian tradition and keeping the memory of ancestral techniques alive, was a desire to preserve the memory of a past which the authorities were trying to suppress by force. A huge canvas by Petrov-Vodkin, *Adam and Eve driven out of earthly paradise,* hangs on one of the bedroom walls. Vladimir, the collector's son, explains that thanks to the relatively privileged position of his family, which enjoyed the exclusive use of an apartment as a perk of his father's job, the collector had been able to purchase some extremely large paintings. These canvases were a good deal cheaper because few art lovers had the space to house them in their apartments! Petrov-Vodkin's debt to the Italian primitive painters, and, in particular, to Masaccio for the frescos in the Santa Maria del Carmine in Florence, is well known. But over and above that undeniable influence, the Russian painter was reviving the iconic tradition. He

1

Portrait of the photographer M. A. Scherling.
Boris Grigoryev. Oil on canvas. 99.3 x 80.5 cm.

rejected the Italian approach to perspective, which gives a false impression of depth at the centre of the painting, preferring, like artists in ancient Russia, to tilt the vanishing point of his composition towards the spectator. In Petrov-Vodkin's painting of Adam and Eve the spectator, instead of becoming lost in illusory distances, can witness the approach of the fallen couple. The large sharply-pointed leaves, the unnaturalistic mountains, are also part of the primitive world of icons where the subject is clearly defined by incisively-drawn lines. Petrov-Vodkin adapts this language to suit the sensibilities of his time. The angel has disappeared, replaced by threatening foliage which forms an impenetrable wall, once again sealing off a paradise which is lost forever. The blues and reds of the old masters have faded, graduating into agitated colours that express the dramatic tension of the scene and the horror of a futile world.

The *Head of Christ* by Kuzma Petrov-Vodkin is another canvas in Paleev's collection. It is overwhelmingly powerful despite

its modest size and Petrov-Vodkin makes use of the symbolic colour scheme, a characteristic of the schools of Novgorod or Pskov. The face is set against a background of crimson, symbolizing divine love, and blue, representing truth. The Holy Face is painted employing traditional methods: a dark colour would have been applied first and then several pale coats would have been added, saturating the base colour with light. In this way, the flesh loses any natural quality it might have had and becomes an image of the transfigured earth, an earth bathed in divine light, the light of icons.

'Roots' and 'memory', are key words in our understanding of the underlying unity of the collector's choices. Even today, spicy odours linger in the air of the apartment where he lived, awakening memories of traditional home cooking. As we sit down to eat in front of a tart filled with blueberry jam, cinnamon perfumes the air as far as the stairwell which has been freshly repainted sky blue. In the kitchen, jars brimming with fruit and vegetables smell sweetly

2

Above the bed, there is a large canvas by Petrov-Vodkin, (Adam and Eve driven out of earthly paradise). Ilya Paleev, due to the size of the apartment where he lived, was able to buy extremely large paintings. These were considerably less expensive because few art lovers had the space to hang them in their homes.

3

Head of Christ, *1927.*
Kuzma Petrov-Vodkin. Oil on canvas. 47 x 35.5 cm.

80

of the countryside and are redolent of past summers spent at the dacha. Nothing seems to have the power to wipe out the past, sustained by so many simple family traditions. Neither the lifeless geometry of the town, nor the political measures intended to obliterate a whole country's memory, can make a people forget its roots. Even the collector's son practises this art of remembering. He is a self-styled curator of the treasures he has inherited. 'Occasionally', he confesses, 'I am tempted to alter the order in which the canvases are hung, to try out a new position. But I always come back to the original layout, the one that my father

contemplated at length. His choices are perfect. The works speak to each other, they are engaged in a private conversation which should not be interrupted.'

Ilya Paleev was not satisfied with merely being an onlooker in the private life of the paintings he collected. He was also friendly with many artists, and in particular, Natan Altman. 'Altman used to come to the house very frequently,' recounts the collector's son, 'and he always used to sit at the same place at the table. On several occasions my father asked him why he had not remained safely in Paris, instead of taking the risk of coming back

84

4
PREVIOUS PAGES LEFT Seated nude, *1928.*
Vladimir Lebedev.
Ink on paper. 51 x 31 cm.

5
PREVIOUS PAGES RIGHT Back view of standing nude, *1927.*
Vladimir Lebedev.
Ink on paper. 35.5 x 24 cm.

6
The Mincer, *1917.*
Vladimir Lebedev.
Oil on canvas. 84 x 56.5 cm

7
Still life with mandolin.
Vladimir Lebedev.
Oil on canvas. 80 x 44.5 cm.

8
The Fortune-teller, *1916. Pavel Kuznetsov.*
Oil on canvas. 69 x 64 cm.

9
Chukowsky's Dacha in the Crimea, *1912.*
Pyotr Utkin.
Tempera, oil on board. 58.5 x 67.5 cm.

86

10
Self Portrait, *circa 1920–30.*
Leonid Chupyatov. Oil on canvas.
71.4 x 60.5 cm.

to Russia. Altman explained that, at the beginning of the thirties, the Spanish Civil War had just broken out and artists and intellectuals had been fired by a boundless enthusiasm. The defeat of the Republicans came as a severe blow to everyone. He said that, in a state of utter confusion, he had trusted the political analyses of his friend, Ilya Ehrenburg. He was living in the Soviet Union, maintained political objectivity with frequent trips to Spain and France and seemed to be well-placed to have a realistic assessment of the situation. But he felt that he was taking advantage

of the trust placed in him by artists in order to encourage them to return to their country to "foil the Bourgeois conspiracy" and oppose the reactionary forces that were raising their ugly head virtually everywhere in Europe. He decided therefore, to come back to Leningrad at the end of 1936 but soon realized the role he was expected to play. On his return, the country's cultural authorities offered to organize a major retrospective of his work and in exchange he was to paint several propagandist canvases and make some statements along the same lines. Natan Altman

11

Real landscapes and stage sets meet on one of the office walls. Views of Versailles painted by Benois mingle with scenes from Carmen by Golovin and the Barber of Seville by Sapunov. At first glance, this might seem to be an eclectic approach, but then the Sun King's Chateau would make the most beautiful setting for an opera. Ilya Paleev also arranged his works to bring out the subtle correspondences and you understand why his son is loath to do anything to alter this hidden harmony.

12

Spring, 1907.
Robert Falk. Oil on canvas. 71 x 62 cm.

88

disappeared from sight and went into hiding with some friends in dachas in the countryside. He preferred to become an outlaw rather than the mouthpiece of a totalitarian regime. In 1942, things quietened down and he was able to show his face again in Moscow and Leningrad. Finally, in 1955, he was awarded the much-coveted title of "Honoured Art Worker of the RSFSR", which guaranteed him a certain material security.' The precarious political life in the former USSR, periods of leniency alternating with periods of repression, account for this extraordinary sequence of events. Altman was treated with suspicion because he was Jewish and because he kept the memory of a past culture alive. His *Catholic Saint* is a good illustration of the art of iconography: the fullness of

the garments with their pronounced folds shroud the body and give the subject a majestic stature. In the eyes of the West, Altman was also living proof of the tolerance shown by the Soviet authorities, who were torn between the desire to wipe the slate clean by eliminating dissenters and the need to present a reassuring image to western Europe.

Altman painted the portrait of Ilya Paleev seated, with a painting in his hands. The collector's son remembers the love his father showered on the works he bought: 'My father never asked what we thought. His choices were governed by intuition. He did not move in the same circles as other collectors, but possessed a scientist's instinct that immediately enabled him to recognize the

90

13
Portrait of Madame Irina Livshits.
Vladimir Lebedev.
Oil on canvas. 66.5 x 52 cm.

best work. Only his friend, S. Block, a Leningrad lawyer influenced him. He did not visit antique shops, which he distrusted, and preferred to buy from the artists themselves, or from their families. At that time, a work by Falk or Altman cost between 500 and 700 rubles. Lebedev, one of his favourite painters, was more expensive and because he was a famous illustrator of children's books you could pay as much as 500 rubles for one of his lithographs. Finding enough money to buy a canvas often entailed financial acrobatics and hardship. But, in the evenings, when my father brought home a painting under his arm, we knew it was a special occasion. He would lay his purchase on the table, gently finger it and wipe it clean with a rag soaked in warm water. Another special moment was when the colours appeared in all their resplendent glory, one of those moments of happiness that helped us put up with the monotony of our day-to-day existence.' Altman's portrait of Ilya Paleev depicts both the piercing gaze of the collector and the unassuming warmth of the man.

Round the steaming samovar, Vladimir Paleev upholds the tradition of family hospitality. He has been content to carry out his father's wishes by reselling a certain number of canvases which the collector was no longer happy with. Today, only one canvas remains still to be sold: a work by Kuzma Petrov-Vodkin, which may seem surprising, in view of the affection that Ilya Paleev had for the artist. The painting in question, however, is a portrait of Lenin.

14
Portrait of Ilya Isaakovich Paleev.
Natan Altman.
Oil on board. 53 x 43 cm.

15
Portrait of the actor Salomon Mikhoels, *1941.*
Robert Falk.
Watercolour. 60 x 45 cm.

16 **17**

Model in the studio, *1901.*　The artist's wife.
Kuzma Petrov-Vodkin.　*Kuzma Petrov-Vodkin.*
Oil on canvas. 59 x 45cm.　*Oil on canvas. 70 x 40 cm.*

92

DIMITRI S. VARCHAVSKY'S COLLECTION

Dimitri Sergeevich Varchavsky has rarely left St Petersburg, where he was born in 1934. However, he can recite the Chinese dynasties from memory and wax lyrical about the rugged mountains in the Yunnan province or the Yangtze Kiang valley. The Orient, an Orient that has disappeared into the mists of time, is his chosen land. All the objects in his fabulous collection of Chinese and Japanese art draw him closer to the countries which he dreams of seeing, one day.

Dimitri Varchavsky was a physics lecturer at the Institute of Education in Leningrad. He discovered his vocation as a teacher during a trip to Siberia, prospecting for mineral deposits. His job allowed him to devote his leisure time to his two passions: his collection and the art of fencing. He achieved a certain amount of success in the latter and became a tournament referee. He admits to being fascinated by ceremonial battle and sports that demand shrewd strategical skill. He considers that fencers, in their white

94

1   2

FROM LEFT TO RIGHT *Incense burner, Tibet; vase decorated with a tortoise, symbol of longevity, Japan; incense burner, Tibet or China; Sino-Manchu Gu vase, Qing dynasty, eighteenth century; lantern in the shape of a house, Japan, nineteenth century.*

Collection of Tsuba. Samurai sword guards (hand-shields), in metal. Japan, sixteenth to nineteenth centuries.

3

OVERLEAF *Dimitri Varchavsky examining his treasures.*

4

The half-light shrouding the apartment brings out the qualities of the lacquer and bronze treasures, gently caressed by the light.

5

Shoulao, god of longevity, is holding a gourd containing the elixir of life. China, Qing dynasty, eighteenth century. ON THE LEFT *Buddhist monk, nineteenth century.* IN FRONT *Soapstone buddhist monk and hermit in the shape of a gnarled root.* ABOVE *Brush box, bamboo, China, seventeenth or eighteenth century.*

6

Large cloisonné vase, patterned with lotus foliage, flowering plants and birds. China, reign of Qianlong, eighteenth century. ON THE RIGHT *Budai, god of earthly possessions, prosperity.* ON THE LEFT *Mythical lion providing structural decoration in pagodas. Southern China, nineteenth century.*

tunics and wire-mesh masks, have a certain amount in common with the Samurai warriors in their articulated breastplates.

For as long as he can remember, Dimitri Varchavsky has been surrounded by objects which evoke the Orient. His father, Sergei Varchavsky, the son of a doctor at the Imperial Court, was himself a collector, passionately fond of lacquer ware and *netsuke*. Dimitri Sergueevitch remembers the fierce arguments his parents used to have when his father came home with a valuable object, to the great displeasure of his mother, who saw her family being financially ruined by this passion. More often than not, these rows would end with the crash of broken porcelain. Young Dimitri and his brother were then discreetly asked by their father to collect up the scattered shards of a Ming vase or a dish decorated with peonies and stick them back together again, behind their mother's back. Dimitri speaks movingly about his father, whose tastes had such a profound influence on him. At the outbreak of the Revolution, Sergei broke away from his family and departed for Moscow where he became an apprentice in a printing works. He

worked as an editor on the Russian Encyclopedia, then as a war correspondent in the forties and finally as an art critic. His most famous book recounts the story of the incredible rescue of the Hermitage collections in 1941, just before the siege of the town by the German troops. *Saved for Humanity* tells of the odyssey of masterpieces by Rembrandt and Titian, El Greco and Velasquez, removed from their frames and boxed up in crates for evacuation from the town. A special train, which was followed by two others, left Leningrad at dawn on 1 July. It was carrying half a million art treasures in 1,118 sealed crates and was heading for the Ural mountains, with a military escort. On 6 July, the armoured train arrived at the station of Sverdlovsk. The sides of the crates, whose contents were unpacked and stored in a secure place, bore the legends: 'coins from the era of Peter the Great', 'Chinese porcelain', 'Italian primitives', 'Imperial silverware', 'Statue of Voltaire by Houdon'. The catalogue of one of the richest museums in the world had been reduced to several hurried labels on wooden crates.

99

7

PREVIOUS PAGES *Bronzes.* TOP *Mouse and dove, Japan, nineteenth century;* RIGHT *Jue vase, China, nineteenth century.* BELOW FROM LEFT TO RIGHT *vase in ancient style; child on a buffalo; divinity, eighteenth century; incense burner; flute player on a buffalo, China.*

8 · 9 · 10 · 11   **12**

Part of the netsuke collection, wood, metal, lacquer and ivory. Japan, eighteenth and nineteenth centuries. The netsuke, kimono accessories used to tighten the cord from which portable everyday objects were hung, were carved in the shape of animals from myth, legend and folklore.

OVERLEAF *Eskimo carvings in ivory and bone. Seals, walruses and whales represent the world of mammal hunting; magic/religious amulets in human form and skeletons with cross motifs reflect the beneficent spirit of Shamanism.*

Dimitri lives in one of the blocks of flats which once housed the palace laundry maids, at the end of the Hermitage Quay, close to the museum whose collections his father helped to save. The bright light which throws reflections of these façades onto the waters of the Neva, dims as the lift, with a dreadful grinding and rattling noise, heaves itself up to the top floor of the house. There is no electricity so groping along the shadowy corridor is a precarious activity. Finally, in a doorway, the lord and master appears and without speaking, courteously ushers one into the dark apartment. As the eye gradually adjusts, the golden gleam

of precious bindings and bright patches of lacquer ware and ivory become visible. This decor seems inspired by passages in Junichiro Tanizaki's *In Praise of Shadows*: 'In contemplating the shadows that lurk behind the highest beams of the room, around a vase of flowers or under a shelf, we sense that a deep silence fills the air in these places and that an eternal peace prevails in the darkness.'

Dimitri Varchavsky has skilfully placed his treasures in settings best suited to bringing out their subtle qualities: an eighteenth-century Buddha sits on top of a cupboard, its unexpected whiteness glowing dimly in the room. The collector

recalls finding it in a shop crammed with bric-a-brac and reminisces about the moment his hands first caressed the white porcelain, because it is with your hands that you come to know an object. With closed eyes you can feel the solid and hollow parts of a carving, trace its rounded contours and explore it with the tips of your fingers. Its substance is hard, yet warm, gradually yielding to your touch. The enigmatic smile that plays across the Buddha's lips seems to be mirrored in Varchavsky's face as he opens drawers and shows off the glistening lacquer work of his *inro*. These small intricate boxes used to hang from a sash and contained medication, ink, tobacco or other small items. In the eighteenth century, their style of decoration was considered to be the height of elegance. But Japanese taste was not only concerned with a stylized and mannered view of nature; inspired by grotesque characters from mythology this art also boasts a popular vein, and the *netsuke* often illustrate this. The word is literally made up of the Japanese characters for 'root' and 'attach'. They were toggles with which men fastened the *inro* or pouch to a cord, indispensable accessories for garments with no pockets. Originally, *netsuke* were made of plain wood, without any decoration, but the sculptors, the

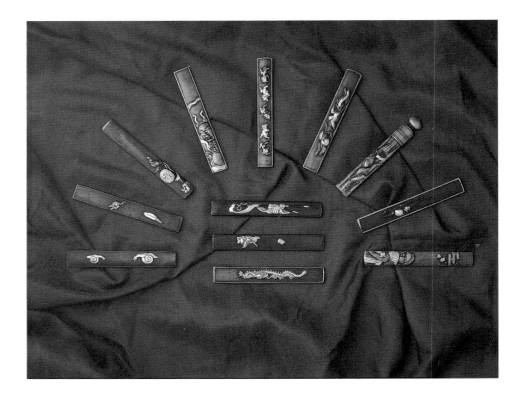

13

Lacquer sword frogs, decorated with gold and silver. Japan, eighteenth century.

14

Samurai sabre blade and scabbard, engraved red lacquer. Japan, eighteenth century.

15

Inro, black and gold lacquer. Japan, end of the eighteenth century. Inro were small boxes which hung from the sash. They were used to carry medication, peppermint, brushes and ink, a pipe and tobacco box, seals and keys.

106

netsukeshi, soon tried to compete with each other's skill in carving ivory, jade or lacquer. It is worth relating how Varchavsky acquired his most enchanting *netsuke* from a shop. On subsequent visits to this shop, he found other *netsuke*, from various periods and intrigued by the regularity of this supply, he questioned the shopkeeper about the provenance of his valuable merchandise. The antique shop owner arranged a meeting with him, which aroused Varchavsky's curiosity even further. On the appointed day, he watched a young woman arrive and unpack several *netsuke*, each one more beautiful than the next. She explained to the flabbergasted art lover that she was a prostitute and that one of her clients, an officer in the Soviet army, paid her with one of these trinkets every time they met. It goes without saying that both the shopkeeper and the collector prayed that this liaison would continue.

Drawers are opened to reveal *tsuba*, Samurai sword guards, whose initial simplicity, like that of the *netsuke*, had been replaced by increasingly decorative elegance. They are made out of a bronze that possesses a certain dark depth and although created for the purposes of war, these elaborate circular objects radiate an overwhelming feeling of serenity. They provide a striking contrast to the 'strangely cloudy' milky jades, which form another part of the collection. But the jade, like the bronze, only comes to

life in the play of light and shadow. A brief flash, sharp as a knife-blade, transfixes a *tsuba*; a pallid gleam is kindled in the depths of the jade which appears to be imbued with 'an age-old spirit'.

The silence surrounding the objects in Dimitri Varchavsky's home is broken only by the visits of young students, artists and specialists in oriental art who come to talk with the collector, who is house-bound due to a physical handicap. They smoke like chimneys and, on special occasions, crack open a bottle of vintage wine. The rows of Buddhas on the shelves watch the coils of cigarette smoke rise, as they would have watched the incense smoke in the temples of Japan. When he is not entertaining visitors, Dimitri devotes his time to studying. He is learning Chinese poetry, and revels in *lü-shih*, eight-line poems in which the poet juxtaposes layers of imagery, discarding syntactical constraint wherever possible. A meaning does emerge, however, from these dislocated fragments, as it does from the collection itself. Objects scattered at random gather in the shadows forming a harmonious whole, dissected by yet more shadows which appear, 'like thin runnels of water trickling over the matting to form still pools; the rays of light are harnessed, one here, another there, then spread out, filmy, uncertain and sparkling, woven on the loom of night like a piece of damask patterned with gold dust.' These words by Tanizaki could be Dimitri Varchavsky's aesthetic bible.

109

16
Teapot in the shape of a Chinese figure symbolizing happiness, porcelain. China, Qing dynasty, eighteenth or nineteenth century.

17-18
Two porcelain vases, one with lid, so-called 'Famille verte' (1662–1722).

IGOR G. SANOVICH'S COLLECTION

1

The suburbs of Moscow, among the inelegant apartment blocks in an area devoid of charm, is where one of the most fascinating collections, Igor Sanovich's, is hidden.

Beyond a tract of wasteland, apartment blocks are silhouetted against the horizon. The estate in the suburbs of Moscow where Igor Sanovich lives is a typical example of Soviet functional architecture. The smell of cabbage and mildew pervades this sinister landscape and accompanies the visitor along the dimly lit corridors and staircases. The door, boasting numerous locks and bolts, opens slowly and you stand aghast on the threshold of the apartment. Igor Sanovich has transformed four tiny rooms into Ali Baba's cave: walls, furniture and floors are enveloped by works of art. In this house, you will not find a traditional approach to hanging, intended to highlight each individual object. Here, paintings are stacked one behind another against a partition,

illuminations are piled in a corner, the drawers are stuffed with antique fabrics, fossils sit next to *netsuke* and oriental vases support dishes, which are themselves overflowing with valuable objects. This place is something like a geode, one of those rocks which enclose amethyst crystals within a crude blackish matrix. In the same way, this dismal suburban apartment block outside Moscow accommodates an unexpected but remarkable collection of curios, comparable to the princely *Wunderkammer* of Dresden or Prague.

Born in 1923, Igor Grigorievich Sanovich worked as a civil servant at the Oriental Institute in Moscow, where his specific job was to study the Iranian labour movement. However, despite this specialization, he has never left his country and his frustrated

111

2

The collector has transformed his tiny apartment into Ali Baba's cave. Oriental fabrics, ancient icons and masterpieces are stacked in his cramped quarters where fabulous objects lurk in every nook and cranny.

ambition to travel is at the root of the sequence of oriental works which constitute the first layer of his collection, his 'humus' so to speak. One of his most beautiful works is the portrait of a young man playing chess, a seventeenth-century watercolour, with gold decoration, painted on gazelle hide. The collector tells of how he pursued this work for thirty years, keeping a watchful eye on it from afar every time it changed owner. Finally, after many years of patience, he was able to buy it, and it is one of his favourite acquisitions. There is something of the hunter in Sanovich as he lies in wait for his prey, displaying a resolute tenacity. Without leaving the narrow confines of his apartment, he follows the peregrinations of works that interest him, as keenly as an eagle. The Persian ephebe is sitting in front of a wall, his garments are embroidered

with delicate pink flowers, a motif which is repeated on the edges of the chessboard at his side. The figure and Sanovich's passion are one, just as the walls of his apartment fade into the background, revealing a secret complicity between collector and his objects. Sanovich refuses to give anything away. His collection is his mouthpiece, an intimate diary, a narrative of suffering for anyone with eyes to see.

As soon as you enter the apartment, your gaze is drawn to a smallish painting, a nude by Laryonov. A woman, half-reclining on a bed, faces the observer. Her brown hair is streaked with indigo, and pink flecks suggest a piece of jewellery on her neck. But it is the butterfly fastened to her foot by a needle that attracts your attention. You are momentarily disconcerted by this sacrilege:

112

3

Igor Sanovich worked as a civil servant at the Oriental Institute in Moscow. His particular job was to research the Iranian labour movement, but he has never left the former USSR. He has seen his compulsory confinement as an opportunity to pursue his epicurean interests.

4

Letters and papers are pinned to the wall next to tools for restoring works. This juxtaposition encapsulates the spirit of Sanovich's entire collection, where his most intimate past is mingled with his desire to give each of these objects a new lease of life; objects which he has coveted for so long and so zealously cared for.

was there really any need to pierce the canvas to attach a worthless bauble? Then it becomes clear that the relationship between the painting and the butterfly is a private symbol. Someone 'flew out' of Igor Sanovich's life, and he admits that he started his collection after this flight of a woman he loved.

Sanovich's oriental works, embodying the dream of an impossible journey, are supplemented by some sixty Russian paintings that span the whole of this century. Falk holds a special place in this second layer of the collection and *The Apples* was the first canvas that the collector bought. Although this still life differs greatly from the young Persian man acquired many years later, they do share certain similarities. There is the same blend of restraint and sensuality, the same balance of cold and warm colours and they both exude the same feeling of melancholy. The two works invite your touch. Your fingers long to caress the smooth surface of the oriental watercolour, to crush the delicate silk of the young

Persian's garment and feel the elegant outlines of the chess pieces. Falk's pieces of fruit, on the other hand, tempt you by the roughness of the picture's surface to which the light clings. Indeed the key to Igor Sanovich's collection is its tactile appeal. The works are not merely contemplative, you have to explore with your eyes and your hands to appreciate the true worth of each object. Before Robert Falk died, in 1958, he wanted to see some of his paintings for one more time. Two of them, *The Potatoes* and *The Apples*, were part of Sanovich's collection. Falk said that all his creative energy had been concentrated in these canvases where the material assumes a life of its own. This is the distinctive characteristic of most of the works chosen by Igor Sanovich. Your finger traces the blue and green arabesques of earthenware tiles, you recognize the same pattern in the flowing lines of a Chinese statuette and your hand delves into the fabrics stored in drawers, fingers the strings of pearls and the gold embroidery.

5
Portraits. *Pavel Filonov.*
Graphite and ink on paper. 22.3 x 22.3 cm.

6
The Church, *1916. Aristarkh Lentulov.*
Graphite and watercolour on paper. 38 x 26.5 cm.

114

116

7
Still life with Pravda.
David Schterenberg.
Tempera on board. 64.7 x 45 cm.

8
Idleness and shadow.
Alexander Shevchenko.
Oil on canvas. 67 x 71 cm.

In the main room, the office and bedroom, three figurines by Tyshler are arranged in a triangle: these are the Dryads. The bodies of the Goddesses have burst free from the bark that had held them prisoner. Wood has become flesh. In the same way, each work seems to escape the collection's rigid constraints in order to begin existing in its own right. The gold of the miniatures, the ivory of the figurines, glow in the half-light of the apartment.

In the twelve-foot-square kitchen, beneath plates from the French Revolution and antique enamel ware, Igor Sanovich concocts superb dinners for seven or eight people. He takes hours preparing pork trotters in aspic, seasoned with aromatic herbs, displaying the same patience as when he is tracking a coveted work. He serves vodka and syrupy Georgian wine in disparate, precious silver goblets. His kitchen also serves as the restoration workshop, where, unlike many collectors, he personally repairs the objects that surround him. Between the heavy old-fashioned refrigerator and the gas cooker, he mends frames, touches up the gilt on an angel's crumbling wing, or reinforces a binding. He values this contact with his works more highly than anything else

and he is a self-styled craftsman. He enjoys finding evidence of the unhurried pace of bygone days among his 'folk art' objects, which form the third layer of his collection. He collects heavy keys and quaint locks in the shape of lions, dragons and birds. In his hands, he weighs the metal which gives things a particular density. In the hall of the apartment, you may be puzzled by a huge cast-iron cockchafer, incongruously set among the paintings and the bunches of dried flowers. Roguishly, Igor Sanovich watches your baffled expression but finally, provides you with the key to the mystery: the insect is a bootjack which comes from the Urals.

This search for authenticity, a quality which is becoming harder and harder to find, prompted him to take an interest in icons. In one of his short stories, *The Sealed Angel*, Nikolai Leskov puts these words into an icon painter's mouth: 'The original idea of noble inspiration has been lost; now they look to earthly things, and their art breathes with earthly passion.' When contemplating the most beautiful piece in Igor Sanovich's collection of icons, the magnificent *Meeting of Joachim and Anne before the golden gates*, you are struck by the attention to detail which gives the

117

9

The twelve-foot-square kitchen doubles as a cabinet of curiosities and a restoration workshop. Igor Sanovich spends long hours repairing, framing and cleaning his treasures beneath a collection of French Revolutionary plates and precious enamel ware. This picturesque den, dominated by an ancient refrigerator, is transformed into a reception room when Igor Sanovich entertains as many as seven or eight guests around the little table. He does the honours at the oven with the expertise of a gastronomic Faust, and serves up, in a tour de force which leaves his guests speechless, pig's trotters in aspic or a tasty goulash in the great tradition of Russian cookery.

10

Annunciation, *sixteenth century. Moscow School.*
Tempera on stuccoed wood. 29.3 x 23 cm.

11

Unlike many collectors, who are satisfied with hanging their acquisitions on the walls to admire them from a distance, Igor Sanovich is more interested in direct contact. He must touch them, caress them, care for them. He therefore keeps virtually all of them within arm's reach, ready to make good the slightest flaw with his skills as a restorer.

120

impression, as Leskov's character says, that each fold, each hair 'has been drawn with a needle'.

Several years ago, in 1978, the apartment was burgled. Sanovich found out later that the theft had been financed by the Home Secretary, Solokov, who was then in power. He was behind a constant traffic of *objets d'art* to western Europe. Scorning the so-called decadent canvases by Laryonov and Tyshler, the thieves made off with eighty icons. Once they had been snatched from this appartment, where the profusion of artistic treasures formed a sort of profane iconostasis, they went on to swell a market that had been developed, in part, by the West's unexpected interest in ancient Russian art. When news of the scandal of these crimes broke and the guilty parties were discovered, Solokov committed suicide. However, even in the face of extortion and deprivation, the collection continues to grow within the grey walls of this suburban apartment block. A living memory hangs on the walls of these cramped rooms, blanking out the everyday world. Letters written in faded ink, pinned to the partition, harness the collector's personal past to the obscure and prestigious history of his treasures. Rings scattered here and there, faded velvet ribbons everywhere – the traces of a long-lost feminine presence persist. Indications of the origins of the collection are buried amongst these precious objects. And in the apartment the fragrance of a woman mingles with the odours of traditional Russian cooking and the sharp smell of drying varnish. Igor Sanovich brings the remembrance of things past to the soulless landscape of present-day Russia.

122

12
Father, mother and son. *L. F. Gegin.*
Graphite and watercolour on paper. 49 x 77 cm.

13
Two female nudes. *Auguste Rodin.*
Graphite and watercolour on paper. 27.3 x 35 cm.

14
The walls in this room are covered with erotic drawings by Rodin and extremely suggestive Chinese prints. Works by Ingres mitigate this ironic choice of decor.

15

Female nude. *Alexander Tyshler.*
Oil on canvas. 75 x 58 cm.

16

Above the sofa, with its cushions covered in Russian folk designs, are several of the collection's major pieces: Apples by Robert Falk, a Female nude by Tyshler and an oriental scene by Kuznetsov. But these masterpieces, instead of being individually displayed, serve as a backdrop for various assorted objects: a Chinese lion sitting on the corner of a piece of furniture, a plaster saint, a bedside lamp. On top of two books, a bronze female nude brushes her raised arm across the sculpted face of the collector, whose effigy dominates the room.

17

Dryad. *Alexander Tyshler.*
Varnished polychromatic wood. H. 75 cm.
Varnished polychromatic wood. H. 63 cm.
Varnished polychromatic wood. H. 56 cm.

18

In front of a watercolour by Drevin depicting a port, there is a pile of mail from people who have been lucky enough to be allowed to leave the country – impossible departures which Tyshler's dryad, imprisoned in her strait-jacket of bark, seems to be dreaming about. Restricted to imaginary trips around his room, Igor Sanovich arranges African stelae cheek by jowl with Asian ivories, worthless souvenirs and postcards from distant lands.

129

19

This cupboard, topped with a bas-relief of glazed plaster, contains rows on rows of ivory and jade carvings. While the putti on the pediment evoke Italy, the treasures on the shelves take us to Egypt and the Far East. This blend is what makes Sanovich's collection so attractive: everything conspires to surprise the visitor with the play of unexpected associations which are always eye-catching and provocative.

20

The huge collection of Japanese prints adds a lighter note to Igor Sanovich's gloomy, cluttered world. The elegant sensuality of the female figures, the sinuous rhythms of the lines and the delicacy of the colours introduce a touch of soothing harmony into this eclectic jumble of objects.

21

Teapot, sixteenth or seventeenth century. Cast-iron, gold inlays, an example of the 'Kiribama' technique. 18.56 x 14 x 11.5 cm.

22

Teapot, sixteenth century. Cast-iron, gold inlays. 14.5 x 16.5 x 13 cm.

23
Young man playing chess.
Iran, seventeenth century. Print on leather,
watercolour and gold. 68.5 x 59 cm.

24
Female nude, *late 1890s. Mikhail Laryonov.*
Oil on canvas. 26 x 38 cm.

25

The paintings pile up, in a succession of layers, against the walls. The Sanovich collection can be thumbed through like a book. This is far removed from the layout of a traditional museum: it is more like a labyrinth, where you can lose yourself in pleasure.

132

26

A ray of light picks out the delicate sphere of a mediaeval ivory in the shadows, some Chinese bronzes, the smile of a Buddha. East and West are unexpectedly united by mysterious harmonies, skilfully orchestrated by the collector.

27 **28**

Two Georgians by a Wine Jar. *Nicolay Pirosmani.*
Oil on oilcloth. 101 x 216 cm.

The Crucifixion and the four Evangelists, *late seventeenth century.*
Silk, embroidered with gold thread. 48.3 x 48.3 cm.

29 **30**

Portrait of a young country girl.
Fyodor Slavyansky. Oil on canvas. 30 x 23 cm.
The painter of this portrait worked for the painter
A. G. Venetsianov who, in 1824, founded an
art school for the serfs on his estate.

The frames touch each other to form a
profane iconostasis which covers the walls,
concealing the shelves of the bookcase and
restricting the amount of room allotted to
everyday objects.

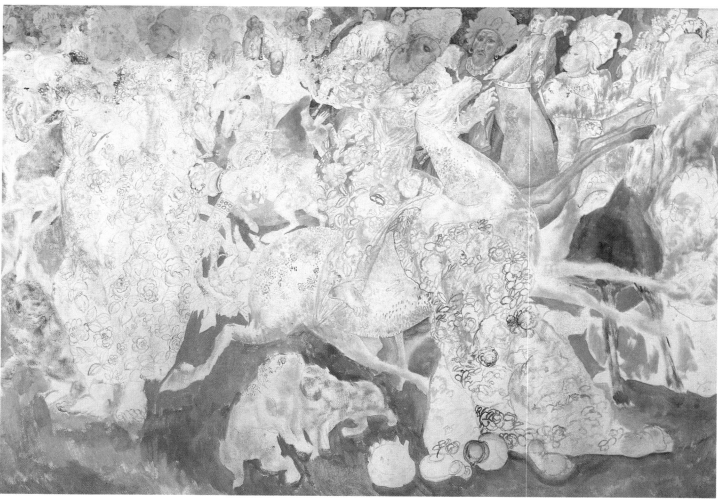

31
Pieces of fossilized wood collected and framed by the collector are surrounded by a miniature bestiary of animal figurines. Some come from the tribes of Chukotka, a province in the far north of Russian Asia.

33
Apples. *Robert Falk. Oil on canvas. 55 x 64 cm.*

32
Horsemen, *1911. Pavel Filonov. Oil on paper. 71.5 x 105 cm.*

34

This tableau is enough to encapsulate the spirit of Sanovich's collection. His personal past, symbolized by this bunch of dried flowers, towers above natural wonders, the disturbing geometries of fossilized wood, and 'kitsch finds' unearthed at the flea market, like the imitation antique ciborium. In the half-light of the apartment, worthless trinkets are placed alongside masterpieces. The eclectic taste of the collector focuses just as much on the inorganic beauty of these pieces of wood, reminiscent of abstract paintings, as on the massive ungainliness of this cheap ciborium.

140

35

The Russo-Japanese War.
Nicolay Pirosmani.
Oil on oilcloth. 107 x 157 cm.

36

Unpolished wooden toys.
Mazin. Nijni-Novgorod, 1920s.

37

Igor Sanovich obviously considers that the numerous locks on his door are insufficient protection of his treasures so he seeks the assistance of a guardian angel, with wings outspread, a simple token of Russian art.

VALERI DUDAKOV'S COLLECTION

142

Valeri Dudakov likes to be thought of as an artist. Born in Moscow in 1945, he studied art and went on to become a successful record sleeve designer. He feels that the high quality of his collection of Russian paintings from the twenties and thirties, which he considers to be one of the best in the country, is attributable to his vocation. Valeri Dudakov has not only inherited the creativity of his grandfather, who was a book binder, he has also been blessed with his father's business acumen. His father, who was a civil servant in the Ministry of Finance, 'had no contact whatsoever with the world of art'. Dudakov's ambition is to reconcile the two traditionally opposed spheres of art and State by giving collectors, whom until now have been constrained to operate in semi-secrecy, an official status. With the support of Raissa Gorbachev, he founded the 'Collectors' Club' in 1987, and then the 'Collectors' Union'. The latter had a broader perspective and aimed at providing a forum for anyone who possessed at least three objects capable of forming a so-called collection. He felt it was important for the Union to have a clearly defined constitution. The machinery of a State agency, even if it is unwieldly, is paramount in safeguarding collectors whom the Soviet regime tended to confuse with all manner of traffickers, thus subjecting them to arbitrary measures and extortion. Dudakov was also behind the great 'Museum of the Twentieth Century' which as yet only exists on paper, but he has not lost hope of one day seeing the project realised and would give the finest pieces in his collection to become its curator. This metamorphosis of collector to curator may seem surprising, but from the time he started collecting, between 1965-70, the young art history student had a very academic approach to the artistic world. He relates how a meeting with one of his professors was formative: 'At the home of Dimitri Vladimirovich Sarabyanov, who was not just a professor but a veritable guru to his pupils, I saw some avant-garde Russian canvases for the very first time. I had been too young when the exhibition, which was a comprehensive survey of banned art from the beginning of the century, took place in 1957 at the Central House of Artists. It was through D. V. Sarabyanov that I discovered Laryonov, Lentulov, Ekster and, most importantly, Lyubov Popova whose spirit and vitality made me realize the true importance of the artistic explosion in the first decades of the twentieth century.' In 1965, Valeri Dudakov was twenty. He had discovered the pleasures of wandering through the picturesque streets of the Arbat, where, not far from Red Square, clusters of antique shops used to sell the inauspicious masterpieces that no museum dared acquire. Dudakov's intuitive recognition of art developed as he walked around and, one fine day, he was amazed to identify a landscape by Robert Falk among the clutter of canvases: 'Out of curiosity I went into the shop and glanced nervously at a view of *Paris, the Seine and a boat.* I managed to decipher the signature: the painting was Falk's work. I knew of this painter through the notorious exhibition of 1958, which had created a scandal when the head of State had walked out, brutally giving the 1922 *Nude* a new title which, in his opinion, was better suited to the "vulgarity" of this "degenerate" work of art: *Naked Valka*. But I also knew about Falk through the many articles that my professor, Sarabyonov, had written about him. I did not buy the Paris scene, but came across it again on a visit to the artist's widow, Angelina Vassilievna. She complained that this landscape had cost her a great deal of money: 450 rubles, but she had made a point of assembling her husband's scattered works. It gave me great pleasure rediscovering the first painting I had ever coveted. To tell you the truth my head swims when I recall all the treasures in those little second-hand shops in the Arbat quarter. There were drawings by Somov, sketches for stage sets by Korovin, canvases by Serov which would be snapped up today, and dozens of Impressionist paintings, all jumbled up together, not to mention many still lifes from abroad from every period imaginable.'

1

Valeri Dudakov with some of his favourite paintings: Portrait of the artist's wife *by Kuzma Petrov-Vodkin, 1922; a* Still life with white roses *by Robert Falk, 1912;* Evening walk *by Mikhail Laryonov, 1907/8; and a painting by Pavel Kuznetsov called* Resting in the Kochara.

The collector had other influential encounters: he made the acquaintance of Glezer, another collector whose tiny apartment was covered with works by banned painters and at his home, he met Oscar Rabin, the guru of the non-conformist younger generation. 'We spent nights in non-stop argument. Long pensive silences were followed by passionate debates which fired our host, a spirited man with a sharp tongue, who sometimes appeared to be highly cultured and sometimes totally ignorant.' One day, Oscar Rabin lent him one of his works, *The Violin* to hang temporarily in his home. 'When it was put up on the wall, Rabin's painting seemed so isolated, so melancholy, that I lost no time in hanging beside it an engraving by Yuri Kupferman (known as Kupfer), bought in Gorki street and an etching that Dimitri Plavinsky had given me. That was the start of my collection.' Dudakov's visit, in 1970, to Vladimir Veysberg's studio in Arbat Street was a third,

important encounter. ' "What do you want?" asked the painter examining me suspiciously. "Have you come to look or buy?" He stressed this last word and I immediately realized that neither visitors or admirers were of interest to him; I pretended to be a buyer. He then asked me point-blank how much I had to spend. Embarrassed, I mumbled something about three hundred rubles, which I did not have on me but could lay my hands on pretty quickly. The artist hastily grabbed his canvases and said abruptly: "Here are some pictures, valued between three hundred and five hundred rubles. When you have made your choice, I will show you some worth one thousand rubles or more." ' Dudakov stopped him and hastily chose the cheapest of the ones he had been offered, *White Geometry*. 'That day marked the birth of my frenzied desire to collect. Veysberg's canvases danced before my eyes. Any one of them could have belonged to me.'

2

Still Life with Blue Carafe, *1912. Natan Altman (1889–1970). Oil on canvas. 76 x 61 cm.*

3

The Tramway, *1914.*
Alexander Bogomazov. Oil on canvas. 142 x 74 cm.

144

Gradually, Dudakov was admitted into the extremely select circle of collectors which possesses its own distinctive code of behaviour and rules. 'I learnt my profession the hard way, and the lessons were often painful. But I was lucky enough to meet someone who introduced me to this corner of the business world and guided me on a journey that was fraught with difficulty. After Sarabyonov and Rabin, my third mentor was Yakov Evseevich Rubinstein, a well-known Muscovite collector who originally came from St Petersburg. I met him at an exhibition called "The Portrait and the Self-Portrait in Private Collections". This was to be the last event organized by the Collectors' Club, which was subsequently banned and which I wanted to revive in the light of Perestroika. One evening, my wife and I were invited to Rubinstein's home in Levchinsky Street. Going through the door of his apartment was like entering a strange and fascinating world. The curtains were drawn and the whole area appeared to be completely inundated with paintings, which covered the walls from floor to ceiling. The best and the worst were hung together indiscriminately. These rooms, lined with pictures, became the haunt of an unlikely gathering. Here the art world rubbed shoulders with crooks, and academics argued with young dilettanti, who might equally well be wealthy heirs or layabouts. Rubinstein never got bored with these get-togethers, and enjoyed the comedy of manners in the same way as he would a show. He had built up his collection after the war. His friends nicknamed him *Kuba*, which, in addition to being a derivative of the name Yakov, was a most appropriate diminutive: each time one of his numerous suppliers offered him something, Yakov would examine each item in great detail with an unerring eye and choose the best, but pay the lowest possible prices. He would even buy things he had no direct interest in and put them to one side as stock (*kubyshka* in Russian), which he could later trade with other collectors. His collection mainly comprised pictures and

4
Portrait of the Artist's Brother, *1933.*
Kazimir Malevich. Oil on canvas. 50 x 40 cm.

5
Three Figures, *1913–18.*
Kazimir Malevich. Oil on canvas. 37 x 27 cm.

146

drawings: masterly works by Laryonov, Tatlin, Goncharova, Lentulov, Mashkov and Petrov-Vodkin were hung side by side with downright daubs. My first exchanges were with Yakov. This practice was, at the time, the best way to build up a collection. Sometimes, we wouldn't exchange just one work for another, but whole sections of wall! We called that type of exchange, "wall for wall". Other renowned collectors would do the same: Gunst, Chudnovsky, Torsouv, Abramyan, Smolennikov, etc. Communal apartments changed owner in this way too. This practice may surprise western collectors, but you must not forget that at the beginning of the seventies, the work of banned painters could be bought for next to nothing. For example, the daughter of Lev Fyodorovich Gegin, a friend of Laryonov and Goncharova, parted with her father's canvases for five or six rubles. Families of artists blacklisted by the regime lived in a constant state of fear. Gegin's daughter, Varvara Tikhonova Gegina, had seen most of her loved ones arrested and deported. She was constantly anxious about her

husband whose only fault was that he had been the son of one of the greatest modern-style architects in Russia. She was no expert when it came to art, but she loved it passionately, with an almost mystical fervour. She lived in one room, in a communal apartment near Crimea Square, where she held gatherings for former pupils of Lev. F. Gegin and Vera Yefimovna Pestel. The room was filled with paintings, which included some magnificent Laryonovs. She was obliged to part with these works in order to survive, and she was only too happy to sell some of those canvases, worth a fortune today, at a ridiculously low price.'

There was another way of acquiring *objets d'art*: this was when major collections of the past were broken up and put on the market, or more accurately, sold off at rock-bottom prices by the collectors' heirs. 'When Vinogradov died in an old people's home at the age of ninety, his heirs notified certain art lovers in strict confidence and, in several days, had disposed of his fabulous collection. Vinogradov, who was one of the heads of the Moscow

6

Valeri Dudakov's home reflects the systematic way in which he has built up his collection. The pale tones of his furniture, in the fifties style which is back in vogue in the West, the meticulous attention paid to the hanging of the paintings and the prevailing order of every room help to create a serene, bright environment. Blue, the collector's favourite colour, continually reappears like a leitmotif, from Altman's Blue Carafe, hung in the office, to the Pre-Raphaelite stained-glass window which is used as a screen in one of the bedrooms. Between the twin beds of the other bedroom, an oval landscape like a porthole opens on to an infinite expanse of sky and sea. And the silvery Night by Dimitri Krymov, a marvellous wood of silver birches bathed in an unreal turquoise light, is set against the backdrop of a blue curtain.

Fine Arts Commission and head of the paintings depot in Moscow, had not only collected works of art. He had held onto everything: *luboks* (naively coloured folk pictures hawked by pedlars all over Russia), coins and even all kinds of tickets. An impressive selection of gingerbread, which had survived the dark years of famine was found at his house and was given to the History Museum of St Petersburg. These disparate objects shared a home with extremely rare pieces, futurist albums by Mayakovsky, precious editions, and canvases by Laryonov and Goncharova.'

Another collection, that of Rossiysky, valued at more than 6 million rubles, disappeared virtually without a trace. It had taken more than half a century for this enlightened art lover to collect unique furniture, hundreds of paintings and countless decorative objects. His fabulous collection of antique pipes also vanished into thin air. 'When a sale was scheduled to take place, possible buyers were discreetly notified. But these were dealers, not collectors, who were more like door-to-door salesmen and fought tooth and nail over this booty, buying it to sell all over the country. This is how vestiges of once famous collections, like that of Blok or Geltzer, came to be found in the furthest reaches of the province. This anarchic situation, which lasted so many years, shows how you could do business, even with a modest income. Today, of course, all that has changed. The little shops in the Arbat, where you had to burrow under second-hand shoes or lift aside rolls of coarse canvas to discover a painting by Falk or Laryonov are long gone. Important western dealers have arrived on the scene. The golden age of collecting is over and we must protect those who have devoted a large part of their time and money to safeguarding the Russian artistic heritage. This was my aim when I founded the Collectors' Union.'

If Valeri Dudakov is to be believed, the garnering activities that went on in the Arbat quarter or the discrete auctions organized by heirs of major collectors were not the only ways of putting together a collection. There was also the recovery of

endangered masterpieces, salvaged from public places. One of the rooms in Dudakov's tiny apartment contains a piece of stained glass which is used as a screen between a child's and grandmother's bed. An angel with outspread wings brings to mind figures from the Renaissance, several flowers picked out against the dark grass are reminiscent of Primitive art and the folds of a piece of brocade seem to have been lifted straight out of a Florentine fresco. However, this stained glass was definitely manufactured in the nineteenth century and is the work of the famous Pre-Raphaelite artist, William Morris. Valeri Dudakov unearthed these broken pieces on the site of a Catholic church which was being demolished in Moscow.

Dudakov's pictures are carefully arranged in rows on the apartment walls, and seem to bear witness to the violence with which art was treated in Russia under the Soviet regime. Kazimir

Malevich's canvases are a poignant illustration, according to Dudakov, of the popular Russian adage 'There is no change without suffering'. He bought two of the three Malevich paintings in his collection from the painter's daughter, Una Kazimirovna. He remembers the 'terse, disjointed' stories she told that conjured up the suffering of a persecuted family whose fate was bound up with the country's tragic history. During the siege of Leningrad, in 1941, Una Kazimirovna snatched a handful of real beans that Schterenberg had incorporated into a still life and ate them. While the *Three figures* of 1913 by Malevich, the founder of Suprematism, display a certain optimism, depicting a vast sky against which the vivid silhouettes stand out, the two portraits painted in 1932 and 1933 express the bitterest disillusionment. The mother's eyes have retained an original innocence which hardship has not been able to undermine. But the portrait of his brother, Mechislav Severinovich

150

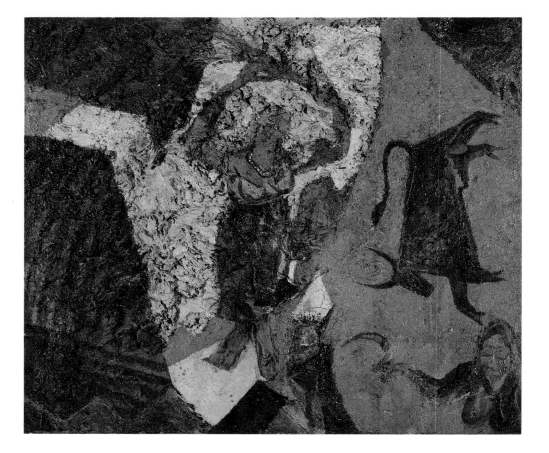

7
Woman reaper, *1914.*
David Burlyuk.
Oil on canvas. 53 x 62 cm.

8
Crucifixion, *1910.*
Aristarkh Lentulov.
Oil on canvas. 71 x 53 cm.

is, according to Valeri Dudakov: 'as cruel and implacable as this period was for our country'. Behind the model with his disillusioned mouth some red streaks symbolize the distant echo of revolutionary dreams. These crimson splashes are an understated reminder of *The charge of The Red Cavalry*, one of the painter's most famous works, a hymn to the irresistible advance of Revolution. When he talks about his pictures, Dudakov stresses their historic context which is of paramount importance. The

judgement of the art historian prevails over personal taste. He says that he does not like some of his pieces, but that he chose them because they are representative of an important period or movement, and are therefore essential acquisitions. His collection is designed to be a retrospective of Russian painting from the twenties and thirties. There is no room for caprice, yet his dream is perhaps not far off: to become the curator of the future Museum of the Twentieth Century.

9

Still Life with Bottle and Pears, *1923.*
Ivan Pouni or Jean Pougny, the name
he took when he lived in Paris in
1923. Oil on canvas. 64 x 44 cm.

10

The collector has arranged a clever setting for a
sculpture by Viacheslav Kolcitchenk entitled Spiral.
The severe geometries of two still lifes, The black
bottle *by Olga Rozanova and* Fruit *by V. Podarsky,*
frame the mellow landscapes and the passionate
lovers by S. Vitberg in On the boulevard. *In this small*
area, art and life, abstraction and realism, meet.

153

YURI WEITSMAN'S COLLECTION

In Yuri Weitsman's spacious living room, the Russian Beidermeier-style furniture is pushed back against the walls beneath judiciously hung paintings and etchings. The centre of the room, whose floor is covered with splendid carpets, remains empty.

The master of the house, attired like a London city gent, shrugs wearily: 'Here, we have plenty of space to entertain, but these days we don't have much to offer our guests.' And yet, it is hard to imagine a more perfect backdrop for sophisticated gatherings. The windows, draped in yellow silk, look out over the ochre palaces of Peter the Great's former capital, not far from the Neva. Yuri Weitsman spent years looking for this ideal setting, which is on the first floor of a splendid colonnaded residence, a

1

In his splendid apartment in St Petersburg, Yuri Weitsman dreams of a revolution in reverse which would boost Peter the Great's former capital and stimulate the growth of an artistic and cultural life comparable to that of western Europe.

2

Portrait of a Girl.
François Boucher.
Black, white and red chalk
on buff paper.
32.5 x 27 cm.

154

3

The Halt of the Horsemen, *seventeenth century.*
Philips Wouwerman. Oil on wood panel. 44 x 64 cm.

4

The living-room is dominated by a full-length portrait
of Catherine II by Jean-Baptiste Lampi.

5

Portrait of the Empress Catherine II, *eighteenth*
century. Jean-Baptiste Lampi. Oil on canvas.
144 x 101 cm. The Empress gestures towards a female
allegory holding a column, possibly a symbol of the
architectural ambitions of the ruler who made St
Petersburg one of the loveliest capitals of Europe.

156

perfect example of neo-classical architecture. In 1969, on his arrival in Leningrad, he lived in a communal apartment where each person was entitled to nine square metres.

He was born in Kiev in 1938 and trained as an engineer. He does not dwell on the story of his lonely childhood, blighted by the death of his mother when he was very young. There was nothing about his background to indicate that this son of a nuclear power station worker would become an enlightened collector of seventeenth-century Dutch paintings and Italian and French drawings. During a business trip he became fascinated by a Dutch painting which he finally bought. 'It was a canvas by Philips Wouwerman entitled *The Halt of the Horsemen*. On entering the shop where it was displayed I was intrigued by the bright patch of sky, and on closer examination discovered, with delight, the intricate detail of the horses and riders. Such refinement was a marvel. As a result of some diplomatic bargaining, I managed to buy the painting for forty rubles. All the same, it was madness, for my salary was no more than a hundred and forty rubles a month. I'd caught the collecting bug and I became a regular visitor to the museums and palaces that were open to the public. I trained myself and am very proud of being self-taught.'

Yuri Weitsman had found the period of art that appealed to his aesthetic ideals and fulfilled his yearning for the past. Seventeenth and eighteenth-century painting provided him with the image of a lost civilization that had constantly haunted him. Philips Wouwerman was his first discovery, opening up a world of amorous intrigue, hunting parties and stately architecture in landscapes inspired by an idyllic Italy. Through studying Dutch painting, Yuri Weitsman discovered the crucial role played by the two rulers, Peter the Great (1689–1725) and Catherine II (1762–1796), in promoting western art in Russia.

Both Peter and Catherine were avid collectors, and in sharing their aesthetic tastes, Yuri Weitsman, with a growing passion, followed in the footsteps of these two great rulers. The

6

Figures beside a Raging Sea, *nineteenth century. Ivan Aivazovski.*
Oil on card. 7.11 x 11.2 cm.

158

capital, built by Peter the Great, is haunted by those cruel and inspired ghosts. Joseph Brodsky, the poet who emigrated to the United States and won the Nobel Prize for literature in 1987, recalls the birth of the imperial city, which became under Catherine II, one of the most beautiful cities of Europe: 'The methods used by Peter the Great to build the city could best be described as conscription. He taxed everything, people and commodities alike, forcing his subjects to bring the land under control. Under his rule, they had very limited choice: they could either be recruited into the army or work on the construction of St Petersburg, and it is hard to say which was the more lethal. Tens of thousands of men died anonymously in the marshlands of the Neva delta, whose islands enjoyed a reputation similar to that of the Gulag today.' Nowadays the city unfurls its vistas and its colonnades along the banks of tamed rivers. In Yuri Weitsman's apartment, the soft light filters through Venetian blinds illuminating a large upright portrait of Catherine II by Jean-Baptiste Lampi

(1751–1830). The Empress makes a grandiose gesture towards a female allegory holding a column, possibly a symbol of the ruler's architectural ambitions.

In Euclidian triumph, great columns on the façades of mansions rose up like organ pipes, stretching into infinity. During the second half of the eighteenth century this city was the meeting place for the best French and Italian architects, sculptors and decorators. To reinforce her imperial image, Catherine was scrupulously attentive to every detail: the granite surfaces beside the rivers and canals and the workmanship of each and every volute on the cast iron railings which run alongside, speak for themselves.

Catherine the Great, nicknamed with good reason the 'Semiramis of the north' after the legendary Assyrian princess, also brought painters and draughtsmen to Russia. Her collection offers a complete panorama of graphic art from the sixteenth to the eighteenth century. As well as Dürer, Callot and Rembrandt the

7
Country idyll, *eighteenth century. Jean-Baptiste Leprince.*
Black chalk, brush and brown and grey wash. 16.5 x 23.8 cm.

159

160

8

Seated figures, nineteenth century.
Guiseppe Bernadino Bison.
Watercolour on paper. 17.4 x 22.5 cm.

9

View of Monplaisir at Peterhof, *nineteenth century.*
Johann Jakob Meyer.
Oil on canvas. 39 x 51 cm.

10

Equestrian Encounter, *1821.*
Jacques François Joseph Swebach.
Oil on canvas. 62 x 50 cm.

11

The windows draped in yellow silk look out over the nearby palaces on the Neva. Yuri Weïtsman spent years looking for an ideal setting to display his collection of Dutch paintings and sixteenth-, seventeenth- and eighteenth-century drawings. It is a far cry from the communal apartments where each person was entitled to nine square metres.

14

Sketch for the costume of King Dodon in Rimsky Korsakov's opera The Golden Cockerel, *1914. Natalia Gontcharova. Gouache on paper. 27 x 16.3 cm.*

162

12

Portrait of the Emperor Nicholas I, *1855. Franz Kruger and his studio. Oil on canvas. 79 x 58 cm.*

13

Portrait of Alexander I, *nineteenth century. Henry Benner. Gouache on ivory, 7.8 x 5.6 cm.*

15

View of Village and Church, *seventeenth century.*
Gaspard Dughet. On the back is a letter from the artist.
Pen and brown ink, brown wash. 7 x 12.7 cm.

16

Sketches: the artist's head, beggar couple, heads of an old
man and woman and beggars' half-length profile, 1632.
Rembrandt, etching. 9.8 x 10.3 cm.

17

Writer in sixteenth-century costume, *also known*
as Man at his Desk with Chain and Cross, *1641.*
Rembrandt. Etching and drypoint. 15.1 x 10 cm.

18

OVERLEAF Massacre of the Innocents, *seventeenth century.*
Attributed to Jacques Stella. Pen, brush and ink, white
highlights on grey-blue paper. 34.5 x 51.5 cm.

168

19

Tsar Nicholas I's autograph.
Verso and end of text: 'In confirmation, we sign
this certificate in our own hand and order for it
to be stamped with our imperial seal.'

20

Tsarina Catherine II's autograph, 1762.
Verso and end of text: 'We certify by our own
signature and by the imperial seal. Catherine.'
Confirmed on 10 October 1762. Chancellor Rioumin.

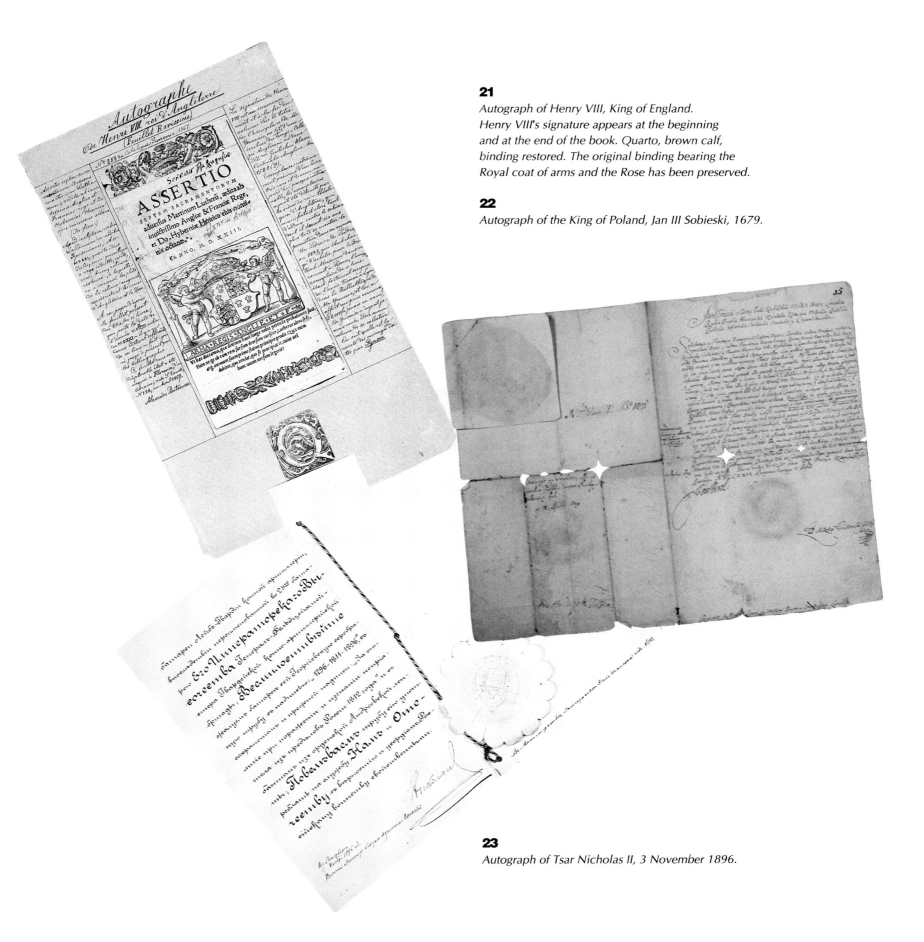

21

Autograph of Henry VIII, King of England.
Henry VIII's signature appears at the beginning
and at the end of the book. Quarto, brown calf,
binding restored. The original binding bearing the
Royal coat of arms and the Rose has been preserved.

22

Autograph of the King of Poland, Jan III Sobieski, 1679.

23

Autograph of Tsar Nicholas II, 3 November 1896.

170

24
Christ on the Cross, *1509. Albrecht Dürer.*
Impression taken from The Little Engraving. *11.8 x 7.4 cm.*

25
Christ in Limbo, *1510. Albrecht Dürer.*
Woodcut. 27.6 x 39.5 cm

26
The Temptation of St Anthony, *1635.*
Jacques Callot. Etching. 35.9 x 45.9 cm.

collection also boasts a *Triumph of Caesar* by Andrea Andreani inspired by Mantegna, and a superb *Massacre of the Innocents* attributed to Jacques Stella. All these works were purchased in St Petersburg. The town harbours countless treasures from looted palaces which are then disposed of through the many antique dealers. Like all Russian collectors, Yuri Weitsman employs a variety of means to augment his collection: bartering, stockpiling objects for exchange and purchasing works being sold off by collectors' beneficiaries. A canvas acquired in this way on the death of a great collector from Khar'kov, Gilmanovich, is going to be sold to finance the purchase of etchings and drawings. His skill lies in knowing exactly when to buy works that others will then be prepared to pay a high price for and in converting these profits into new additions to his own collection. This task is often hampered by a lack of regulations, typical of Russia. More than anyone else, Weitsman dreams of a market based on western principles, and

171

envisages retrospectives and catalogues being drawn up in collaboration with the museums. For the time being, however, this remains a dream. No collector is prepared to leave anything to a museum: they all know that their treasures are bound to gather dust in the vaults for ever with no proper cataloguing system. A well-organized market and effective laws would have prevented an unfortunate incident which befell him in Khar'kov. He met an elderly lady there, aged eighty-five, who wanted to sell a seventeenth-century painting. Her asking price fluctuated between 2,500 and 15,000 rubles. They finally agreed on a figure. But the next day, at dawn, the lady came hammering on the door of Weitsman's room, rousing the neighbours and screaming that he was a thief. Having slept on it, the worthy octogenarian already regretted letting the painting go for too low a price.

Until the laws on private property are reformed, until Saint Petersburg truly becomes Peter the Great's 'window on to the West', a dream that Weitsman shares, he will live in solitary isolation with his treasures. The autographed letters from Tsars Nicholas I and Nicholas II, the decrees signed by Catherine II are shown only to a few rare visitors.

For Yuri Weitsman, reviving the past is an inspiration for the future, rather than an excuse for mere nostalgia. But resources must be made available if the 'openness' once experienced under more enlightened regimes and now dreamt of in the light of *Perestroika*, is to be realized. Poised between two worlds, Yuri Weitsman is symbolic of this ambiguous state of affairs: he is currently preparing an exhibition about the Romanovs, intending that it should tour Europe, and he is making his sixteen-year-old son study art history. Everything is ready, the scene is set, but when will his secret dream come true? When will his white-columned mansion become a gateway to the Europe of the connoisseurs?

27 **28**

Boy Burning a Dead Branch, *eighteenth century.* River Landscape, *seventeenth century.*
George Morland. Oil on canvas. 48.5 x 60.7 cm. *Salomon Van Ruysdael. Oil on canvas. 55 x 82 cm.*

29   **30**

The De-louser, *seventeenth century.* Adriaen Van Ostade. *Oil on wood panel. 29 x 34 cm.*   Village Scene, *seventeenth century. David J. Teniers, known as the Younger. Oil on wood panel. 22 x 28.2 cm.*

174

31

*In the famous Tula workshops, arms manufacture went hand-in-hand with that of
precious metal objects from nineteenth-century gun metal. This service, displayed on a
Louis XV inlaid table, bears witness to the elegant lifestyle of the owner.*

32

When generals were victorious in battle, they were given these plates bearing their emblem.
The plates were made in the imperial workshops of St Petersburg and date from the same period
as this elegant reproduction Reisener table, from the end of the eighteenth century.

ABRAHAM F. CHUDNOVSKY'S COLLECTION

1 - 2

The apartment block where the Chudnovsky family lives is in the so-called 'intellectuals' district' of St Petersburg. There is no point ringing any of the bells, as they are purely decorative and rarely work. As always, a symphony of smells pervades the staircase, a combination of cabbage soup, noxious disinfectants and cat's urine. The lift has not operated since some inconsiderate visitors recently walked off with all the machinery, which they dismantled piece by piece.

The apartment block in the so-called intellectuals' district of St Petersburg is built around a large, gloomy, square, central courtyard. The Chudnovsky family's apartment is on the top floor. There is no hope of taking the lift: all the machinery was recently dismantled by thieves who probably sold the parts on the black market. A huge refrigerator, in keeping with the massive architecture stands in the hall and paintings are stacked next to it. This surprising juxtaposition reveals the main preoccupation of those who live there: survival. They amass provisions in case of a shortage and collect masterpieces to combat the cultural repression of the Soviet regime. It was for this reason that Abraham Chudnovsky, a renowned physicist, collected some two hundred and fifty works which constitute the biggest private collection of pre-war Russian painting.

Abraham F. Chudnovsky was born in 1910 at Elisavetgrad in the Ukraine. He died in 1985 in Leningrad. The memory of the collector is kept alive in the apartment shared by Yevgenia Chudnovsky, his widow, his son Felix and the latter's wife and two daughters, Irina and Katia. In his study, Abraham's photograph is surrounded by freshly cut flowers, a supreme luxury in these times of deprivation, and, in accordance with Jewish tradition, a few modest offerings, buttons and amber beads have been arranged in a little dish. A still life by Osmyorkin and an urban landscape by Lentulov are hung behind the photograph. These two paintings typify Chudnovsky's attitude to collecting. In 1910, Aristarkh Lentulov was one of the founder members of the group of young painters who called themselves the 'Knave of Diamonds'. This pseudonym was the symbol of a group of artists who were breaking away from the prevailing aesthetic conformity. Lentulov and his friends invited the Fauves and the Cubists to their major exhibition in 1910. They tried to adapt Cézanne's lessons to Russia's oriental sensibility.

178

3

*The Chudnovsky family: LEFT TO RIGHT Katia, Irina,
standing beside her mother, then Yevgenia Chudnovsky
and her son, Felix, who is a very well-known scientist.
He is the only man in this all-female environment.*

4

At Table (Easter). *Pavel Filonov.
Oil on paper. 37 x 47.5 cm.*

5

Portrait of a Man, *1947. Vladimir Tatlin.*
Oil on panel. 47 x 32.7 cm.

6

This room sometimes serves as a guest-room for overnight visitors who, deep in conversation, have lost track of the time. The bridges which link the different districts are closed at night. Above the armchair, a pink and yellow bouquet by Alexei Jawlensky, one of Kandinsky's friends during his exile in Munich. On the bookshelves is poetry, especially by the Symbolists. Culture provides the backdrop for daily life and is inextricably bound up with everyday preoccupations.

7

The Sweeper, *1914–1915. Marc Chagall.*
Gouache on paper. 28 x 24 cm.

180

8

Yevgenia Chudnovsky, the collector's widow, sits in the Russian Biedermeier-style drawing-room in the flat she shares with her son Felix and his family.

9

Each room serves as a bedroom, library, drawing-room and exhibition area. Katia, one of Felix Chudnovsky's two daughters, is currently studying in the United States and does not plan to return to her native city.

10-11

The kitchen is the heart of the house. It is where its occupants take refuge to read in the early morning or late into the night. When all the other rooms are taken up by the sleeping family, friends are entertained in the kitchen around a samovar and many hours are spent putting the world to rights. Professor Felix Chudnovsky, the collector's son, likes to retreat there to read his newspaper under a portrait of himself as a young man by Ninas Avetician, a friend of his father's.

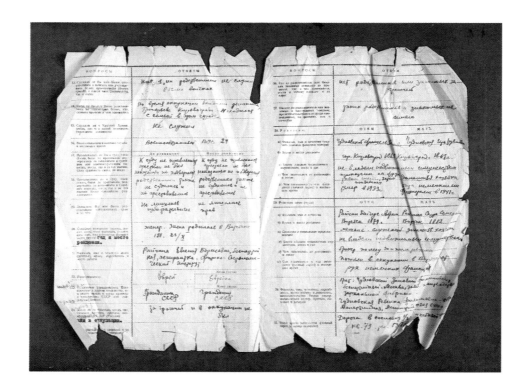

184

12-13

When interrogated by the authorities, Abraham Chudnovsky managed to maintain a cautious silence to protect his family. 'Did you or your family serve in the White Army?' 'Neither I nor my family served in the White Army.' 'Did you serve in the Red Army?' 'No.' 'Who among your family and friends has left the country? When and why? Give details of their profession and their address.' 'I have no friends or family abroad,' replied Professor Chudnovsky although one of his relatives had emigrated to the United States. Under a dictatorship, lying is one of the best forms of resistance.

14

Beside the collector's photograph, in a small glass bowl, a devoted hand has placed buttons and beads. This humble offering acts as a faithful memorial to the past, while on the walls of the apartment the rows of paintings keep alive the memory of the man who assembled them.

The emblem they adopted, the Knave of Diamonds, symbolizing a promise of pleasure, illustrated their desire to instigate a revival of ethnic Russian painting, which had become restricted to imitating academic models directly based on what was considered to be western good taste. Osmyorkin was one of the last members to join the Knave of Diamonds group.

These two paintings do more than reveal Abraham Chudnovsky's fondness for this particular period. The physicist seeks to express the fundamental laws of the universe, just as the artists sought to make the essence of the objects they painted perceptible. Thus, the solidity of factories and apartment blocks, the facets of a glass or the folds of a curtain are pared down to the essential. This evokes the basic philosophy of Albert Einstein, whom Chudnovsky admired enormously. Einstein claimed that in order to achieve the maximum effect one should aim for the greatest simplicity in the demonstration of scientific fact. And this is precisely what the two Knave of Diamonds painters did. The world appears as a conglomerate of simplified matter, where colour

assumes extraordinary intensity. It does not matter that Lentulov's factories are too red or that Osmyorkin's carafe has an imperfect finish. 'Naturalism is not synonymous with realism, that is what is inside you, in the heart,' said Chagall, from whom Abraham Chudnovsky bought two paintings, *The Sweeper* and *Lovers in pink*. The artist's intuition is similar to that of the scientist and towards the end of his life, Chudnovsky tried to analyse the relationship between physics and painting, writing an essay about it. He felt that the painter in the projection of his personal vision on to canvas has much in common with the scientist who suddenly discovers that his scientific reasoning confirms his original intuition. A similar type of insight, enables the artist to choose the forms and colours best suited to express his perception of things and the scientist to outline his findings.

Abraham Chudnovsky liked quoting Chekhov on this subject: 'I think that an artist's intuition is sometimes equal to a scientist's brain, and that they both have the same goal, the same nature. Perhaps with time and progress, both are destined to

15
The Cook in white. *Robert Falk.*
Oil on canvas. 115 x 73 cm.

16
Apples and Eggs, *1921. Kuzma Petrov-Vodkin.*
Oil on canvas. 36 x 47.8 cm.

187

become one and the same, merging to form a colossal force which we are not yet able to imagine.'

Painting stimulated the physicist to reflect on his own work. It is understandable that he had a preference for artists working at the time of the scientific revolution at the turn of the century. 'These artistic movements,' he cried, 'played a similar role to the relativity and quantum theories. The same spirit rid us of a backward-looking naturalistic vision of the world. The same intuition revealed to us the secret harmony of the universe, constant but ever shifting.' The painters of the Knave of Diamonds group borrowed from Cézanne an unswerving fidelity to motif, but they brought it to life with splashes of colour that showed the

movement of the brush. Abraham Chudnovsky chose works that bore witness to that development. A splendid still life by Mashkov is very much inspired by Cézanne. The corner of the table cut off in the foreground and the heavy curtain in the background are typical of the French painter. But introduced into Cézanne's 'harmonious relationship of forms' (Henri Perruchot) are notes of colour that do not break up the visible into patches of light and colour in the manner of the Impressionists, but serve as highlights, on the skin of the pumpkin, on the side of a carafe or on the leaves of an artichoke. Another still life in this collection, by Konchalovsky, takes this process even further. The positioning of the objects is thrown into disarray by the use of colour, everything bursts out of

17
Still Life with Oranges, *1958.*
Vladimir Veisberg.
Oil on canvas. 73.7 x 87.8 cm.

18
Photograph on the Wall,
circa 1920–1930. David Shterenberg.
Tempera on canvas and collage. 61.8 x 40.5 cm.

188

its confines and objects placed at different angles to the light begin to dance. Accentuated with blue, Konchalovsky's still life transforms the apparent chaos of things into a brilliant ballet, and the discovery of the secret choreography of a work is a source of great spiritual satisfaction. A chance intuition coincides with the painter's intentions. For the artists of the Knave of Diamonds group, creativity could only result from this mixture of risk-taking and effort, of carefree defiance and decisions taken after much thought.

The Chudnovsky collection also represents a revival. The collector was not content merely to seek intellectual complicity with his favourite artists. He drew from them the strength to continue, to resist. Becoming a collector was his affirmation of hope. On 5 March 1953, Joseph Stalin died. The following day, the

scientist bought his first painting. He felt that the painter, Robert Falk, who was the founder of the Knave of Diamonds group, embodied this silent resistance to the regime. The Chudnovsky collection includes a few masterpieces by this severe, honest artist, who, as an old man was brought to the Chudnovsky's home one evening. He was asked to paint the portrait of Yevgenia Chudnovsky, but flatly refused. He said he would be happy to paint the professor, but since the artist lived in Moscow and required his subject to sit for a number of hours, Falk's portrait of Abraham Chudnovsky never materialized.

Both artist and collector possessed the same attitude towards the communist regime: they were acquiescent but did not submit. Falk was a member of the Union of Russian Artists, which

19

The photograph of Abraham Chudnovsky, who died in 1985, is surrounded by freshly cut flowers, a luxury nowadays in Russia. Behind this portrait, two paintings by Osmyorkin and Lentulov demonstrate the collector's admiration of painters of the Knave of Diamonds group.

20

Pitcher against a Pink Background, *circa 1919.*
Alexander Osmyorkin. Oil on canvas. 75 x 62 cm.

190

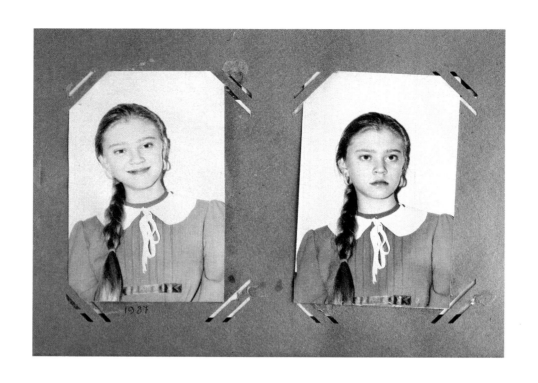

guaranteed him decent accommodation and the means to obtain the necessary materials. In exchange, the artist's work was checked by inspectors to ascertain that it was not in any way subversive or decadent and remained faithful to Socialist Realism. Falk also had to undertake official commissions, which he did, but not without effrontery. One day he was ordered to depict a procession in honour of the regime – he painted a funeral. Similarly, Professor Chudnovsky agreed to play the game for the sake of appearances. He accepted the official duties which ensured a decent life for his family and in addition to an individual apartment he was given a *dacha* with a vegetable garden, providing them with a better than average standard of living. But day after day, defying the official party line, he hung works of art on the faded wallpaper. For him it

was the collection that made the difference between bitterness and pleasure, between the difficulty of everyday life and inner joy. Robert Falk's portraits fulfil a similar need. They are half-way between realist chronicle (the double portrait of his parents dressed up in their Sunday best) and pure aesthetic pleasure (the red dress in *Portrait of the artist's wife*). Behind *The Cook in white*, seated and idle, whose face betrays all the disillusioned weariness of the world, Robert Falk painted a still life. With a few touches which transcend the grim reality, the artist shows us the peaceful beauty of 'inner life'.

Abraham Chudnovsky forged a close friendship with another painter, Natan Altman, and his wife. Altman refused to submit to the censorship of the authorities so did not benefit from

21 - 22

Katia, the schoolgirl with the thick plait and a demure collar, could not resist the lure of foreign parts. She chose the United States in preference to the apartment lined with extraordinary paintings but where the simplest telephone call requires hours, even days of waiting.

23

The Composition (One composition on the shoulder of another), 1918. Yuri Annenkov. Oil on canvas. 92 x 65 cm.

193

24
Portrait of Nadezhda Dobychina, *1913.*
Natan Altman. Oil on canvas. 85 x 61 cm.

25
Nadezhda Dobychina, *whose portrait by
Altman is one of the prizes of the Chudnovsky
collection, patronized all the artists persecuted
by the authorities. In 1906, at her St
Petersburg apartment, she exhibited Chagall,
Kandinsky and Altman. Chudnovsky seems to
have taken up the torch lit by this brave
defender of what was judged to be 'decadent
art'. The blue and grey tones of the portrait
contrast with the oriental-style decor, the
brightly coloured fabrics and the art nouveau
lamp, its shade decorated with gems
(cabochons).*

26
Fishes, *1903–1906. Mikhail Laryonov. On the
back is an inscription by the painter in Cyrillic
script: 'Exhibiting this painting is prohibited'.
Oil on canvas. 64 x 73 cm.*

any of the privileges enjoyed by official artists. Shortly before his death in 1970, a retrospective of his work was organized in Leningrad and when journalists asked what his official title was, the painter replied: 'Just write my name. That is enough.' Chudnovsky owned two magnificent portraits by Altman: one of Nadezhda Dobychina, a variation on cold tones, and the other, the *Negress* in a red and gold dress. Altman is a virtuoso in his use of colour. It is a means of expression for him and he does not play with it to introduce movement into his compositions, like the Knave of Diamonds group, to which he never belonged. The model's pallid face and steely gaze in the *Portrait of Nadezhda Dobychina* echo the sober grey and black decor, while the intricate work on the blouse and the stylized blue flowers of the curtain suggest a dreamlike atmosphere, transcending all resignation. The *Negress*'s vivid dress is imbued with a warm exoticism which has been lost for ever.

Abraham Chudnovsky's taste prompted him to choose paintings where the colours themselves became a language. He liked the works of Kuzma Petrov-Vodkin and bought his famous still life which depicts four apples and two eggs against a completely blue background. It is understandable that the scientist appreciated the discipline of these perfect forms set against this hue, symbolizing infinity. Of modest proportions, Petrov-Vodkin's work conceals an unfathomable secret. The simple magic of the colour gives it a vertiginous depth. Petrov-Vodkin's humble apples resemble spheres revolving in the cosmos while the eggs represent perfect miniature trajectories of entirely mathematical purity. Madame Chudnovsky tells how her husband acquired another of the artist's works, a huge portrait of a woman. Petrov-Vodkin, who died in 1939, had never placated the authorities so his widow only qualified for a communal apartment shared with nine other families. Chudnovsky purchased from her other paintings that are

195

196

27

Masterpieces, family photographs, precious and not-so-precious objects bear silent witness to the lives of the apartment's occupants. Some of the works are intimately bound up with their owners' personal history. Chagall's Lovers in Pink *celebrates the passionate love at first sight which was kindled one morning in 1932 between two young people queuing to buy a train ticket. Abraham and Yevgenia were married eight days later, and remained together for fifty-three years. It was this symbolic painting that their son Felix saved in 1978 when thieves broke into their apartment in search of the works of Chagall, whose market value had made them highly coveted prizes among the higher echelons of government.*

28

Portrait of the Artist's Parents. *1911. Robert Falk.*
Oil on canvas. 108.5 x 87.5 cm.

29

Lovers in Pink, *1916. Marc Chagall.*
Oil on card. 69 x 55 cm.

30

*In the drawing-room, the cold light of the St Petersburg
sky is reflected on the bleached birch parquet floor. The
striped wallpaper has not been changed for forty years,
for want of materials and tools to renovate it and also
perhaps because it is too daunting a task.*

31

*Still Life with Japanese Print, 1911–1912.
Pavel Kuznetsov. Tempera on card. 73 x 96 cm.*

included in his collection. She lived in a room that was divided down the middle by her husband's paintings. She shared a kitchen and the only 'bathroom' – a cold-water tap and a basin behind a curtain – with the other tenants. As all commerce was banned, it took a certain amount of cunning to remove the paintings from the apartment. The size of the portrait made things difficult. The neighbours would have had no hesitation in reporting the painter's widow to the militia so Abraham Chudnovksy turned thief: he stole into the apartment by night and carried off the carefully wrapped painting.

Collecting always verged on the illicit, and the semi-clandestine activities that all collectors engaged in exposed them to all sorts of demands. Like Igor Sanovich, Chudnovsky had the dubious honour of attracting the attention of high-ranking officials who seized some of his treasures. The crooks, financed by the Party's top officials operated in broad daylight, feeling sufficiently protected to act with complete impunity. Felix Chudnovsky describes how the theft took place: 'When they rang the bell, that day in 1978, I was alone in the flat and I didn't open the door. They rang again and I went over to the door. Before I realized what

199

32
Monumental Head, *1910–1911*.
Kuzma Petrov-Vodkin. Oil on canvas. 132 x 96 cm.

33
Spring in Town, *circa 1910–1911.*
Natalia Goncharova. Oil on canvas. 69 x 97.5 cm.

was happening, the door was smashed to pieces with a terrible crash and four men threw themselves on me, bound and gagged me and left me on the settee in the drawing-room. I was able to watch the comings and goings of the thieves and I quickly realized that they did not know what they were looking for. One of them ripped off my gag and shouted: "Where's the Chagall?" He was standing over me, but I merely replied: "Look for it." As they insisted, and became threatening, I sent them over to another painting, in my father's study.' In the end, his attackers walked off with twenty-three paintings, works by Malevich, Goncharova,

Laryonov, Tatlin and other important artists. When his parents returned, they lodged a complaint against the authorities. A few days later, the militia brought back eleven of the stolen paintings, without bothering to give a word of explanation. But the others never resurfaced. This robbery was a serious warning from the authorities. However, the family later learned that the person behind this episode had ended up committing suicide. The Brezhnev years were the toughest for the collectors, who found themselves at the mercy of the whims and greed of the highest officials in the regime.

203

34   35

Lisa in an Armchair (Portrait of the Artist's Wife). *Robert Falk. On the back, an inscription in Cyrillic script: 'Portrait of E.E. Potekhina, the artist's wife'. Oil on canvas. 100 x 80 cm.*

Poppies. *Natalya Gontcharova. Oil on canvas. 74 x 73 cm.*

Today, in the St Petersburg apartment furnished in Russian Biedermeier style, the warm welcome and the lengthy discussions around the samovar partially erase these dreadful memories. Everywhere, the paintings patiently acquired by Abraham Chudnovsky evoke the tragedy of the past but keep hope alive. A brightly-coloured telephone sits on the refrigerator in the hall. Every year, they tell us, the colour is different, yellow, blue, it used to be red. Those days are over. So many telephones, but their colour is unimportant when there is no dialling tone. Colours may come and go, but the line remains silent.

Abraham Chudnovsky's collection represents the perfect marriage of art and science. His passion for painting was not merely a distraction which helped him forget his work. Art confirmed the scientist's theories. Just as the painter turns alchemist in shaping matter and mind, the physicist becomes an artist when his most abstract speculations confront the truth of the tangible world.

205

36   37

Family Portrait *(from the series* My childhood neighbours*).*
Alexandr Tyshler. Oil on canvas. 82 x 62 cm.

Negress, *1930.*
Natan Altman. 91 x 61 cm.

MIKHAIL PERCHENKO'S COLLECTION

1

Mikhail Perchenko began his collection by chance when he was strolling around the Arbat, the antique dealers' district around the Kremlin. His apartment, in a beautiful eighteenth-century residence, is bursting with treasures. He confesses a preference for furniture and glassware, and has a keen interest in the Italian Renaissance.

2

The skilful balance of different styles makes you feel as though you are entering the apartment of an old Russian aristocratic family rather than a private collection. There is no didacticism in the way the objects are displayed and a fine harmony and elegance are always evident.

We are in a wide, leafy avenue lined with what were private mansions which now house numerous embassies. This tranquil, pleasant district seems a far cry from the tumult of Moscow's centre, where dense crowds jostle the stroller and where the air is thick with smoke and dust. On entering the beautiful eighteenth-century residence where Mikhail Perchenko lives one experiences a few fragrant surprises. The smell of wax polish replaces the customary odour of cabbage and cats which permeates staircases throughout Russia. This is because our host feels duty bound to shoulder the maintenance costs for the communal parts of the building, which he wants to reflect his aspirations and live up to his collection. The impression of being a long way from the realities of Moscow grows as you enter his apartment, which occupies half a

floor. These rooms, bursting with European treasures and antiques could be in Vienna or Munich. Proud of the aristocratic origins of his wife Helena, a descendent of a family which goes back further than the Romanovs, Mikhail Perchenko presents himself first and foremost as a European, at the confluence of several cultures, and this is reflected in his collection.

How did he begin? By chance, walking through the Arbat district, on the way to the school and conservatory where he began his musical studies at a very young age. His parents had plans for him to pursue a musical career. He was to be a violinist. During his studious childhood and adolescence, his wanderings through the Arbat provided a glimpse of a world of luxury and beauty. Soon all the antique and second-hand dealers got to know him. Every shop

3 **4**

Portrait of Countess Vassilievna Skavronskaya, née Engelhardt. *Elisabeth-Louise Vigée-Lebrun. Oil on canvas. 79 x 65 cm.*

Miniature. Gouache on ivory.

208

window seemed to contain the mysterious promise of escape. He bought his first curios at the age of fifteen: porcelain figurines whose refinement evoked a past that fuelled his imagination. This hobby soon became a passion: 'I was intoxicated,' he says, 'by the atmosphere of discovery and bargaining. I immersed myself in books to learn more about my finds. I had to abandon my music studies because my wrists broke as a result of the intensive training, so I gave myself a year to think about my future. I studied a little and devoted myself to my passion. Then I took up psychology and for a while I practised at the Moscow psychiatric hospital and that was when I had the time to begin collecting seriously and systematically. I picked up icons, from different eras and places but it was a risky business. The interest western collectors took in icons, for which they were prepared to pay dearly, presented a danger for us. Certain top government officials had no hesitation in resorting to all sorts of means to confiscate these objects for their own benefit. Robbery and blackmail were their usual methods. I was spared as, after 1975 I sold my icons, with the exception of my three favourites: *The Raising of Lazarus*, from the Novgorod school of the sixteenth century, an eleventh-century Byzantine work and one from the Dionysian school. With the profits from this sale, I threw myself wholeheartedly into a new collection, concentrating on the furniture and decorative arts of Peter the Great's period. To the paintings, porcelain and glassware, I added Dutch art, which the Tsar loved. I confess I have a passion for furniture, both Russian baroque and English Chippendale.'

These eclectic tastes do not detract from the overall unity: Perchenko's apartment is evocative of an ancient aristocratic tradition rather than the contemporary frenzy of a collector. Here the past is a heritage, not a mere acquisition. The arrangement of the objects and their skilful combination defying chronological constraints creates a charming atmosphere. There is no didactic

5

Portrait of Count Dimitri Tatichtchev, *Russian ambassador to Vienna, painted circa 1820. Mikhail Daffinger Moritz. Gouache on ivory. Its counterpart,* Portrait of Countess Julia Tatichtcheva, *is in the Russian Museum in St Petersburg.*

6

Miniature. Gouache on ivory.

209

7

The oldest pieces in the collection, dating from the seventeenth century, come from the Izmailovo workshop (a small village in the suburbs of Moscow), which was founded by Italian master glass makers from Murano, invited to Russia by Peter the Great's father, Tsar Alexei Mikhailovich.

8

This iridescent vase is one of the fragile treasures which vibrates to the touch and sparkles when caught by the slightest ray of light.

210

9-10

OVERLEAF *A few examples of the many pieces of glassware in the Perchenko collection. Next to the first engraved glasses are stemmed glasses decorated with gold, silver or platinum designs and with views of St Petersburg. The ruby, amethyst and sapphire coloured glasses appeared at the very beginning of the eighteenth century, when metals were used to create the different tints.*

11

At the time of Peter the Great, western master craftsmen were invited to Russia to manage the factories. The first glass, stone and carpet factories were founded then and reached the height of their glory during Catherine the Great's reign. Part of this collection of white opaline shows that these delicate little French pictures appealed to Russian taste.

12

These elegant white seventeenth- and eighteenth-century engraved glasses had little chance of surviving. During the course of a dinner, at least fifty to a hundred would get broken. It was only after the contents of the Tsar's storehouses were sold off in the twenties and thirties that they were put on public display and acquired by private collectors.

215

13

Imaginary landscape. *A rectangular faience plaque. Decorated in Spanish emerald greens, yellow-orange and pale blue. The balance of the firing colours was crucial for the seventeenth- and eighteenth-century painters of Castelli. Two families of painters, Grue and Gentile created faience depicting such figurative scenes based on sixteenth-century engravings.*

14-15

Collection of Italian majolica from Urbino, Venice and Faenza.
BELOW *Italian majolica pitcher.*

217

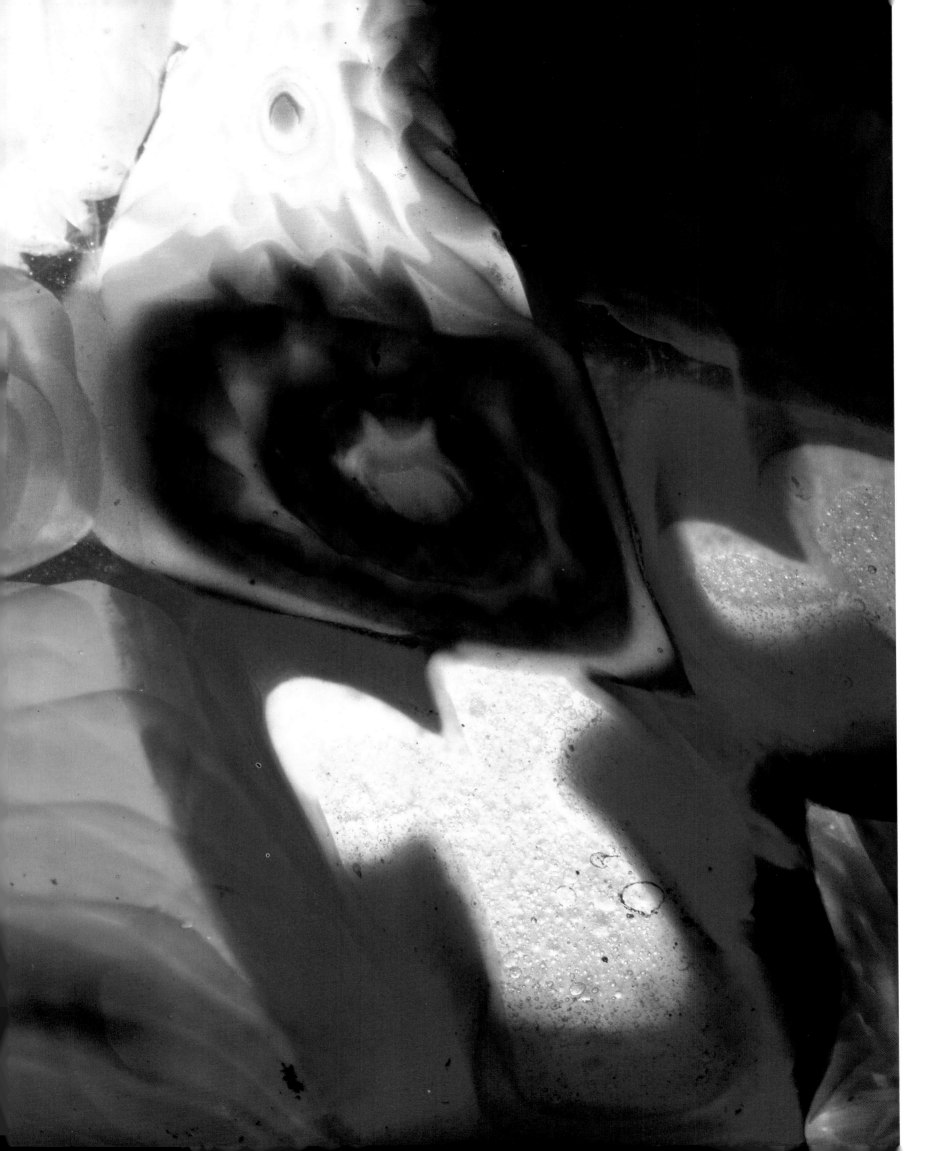

220

16-17

PREVIOUS PAGES *Early nineteenth-century 'Millefiori' vase in Murano glass. This technique for making brilliantly coloured glass was developed between 1820 and 1830.*

18

This eighteenth-century bureau cabinet in Baltic pine was acquired from a Moscow palace. It houses a small part of the collection of eighteenth- and nineteenth-century decorative art in steel, bone and ivory.

19

These caskets, boxes, goblets and candle holders were made in the Tula factory, famous for its firearms with finely chased barrels. The matt appearance of the neglected silverware sets off its delicate decorative carving. The rarest pieces are in brown steel and gilt. Royal education demanded that male heirs learnt a manual trade and turning artistic pieces was a favourite choice. Thus Peter the Great devoted himself to the art of turning ivory or bone chandeliers. These few pieces from a large collection of caskets, little pictures, frames and other curios from the Golden Age illustrate the importance of the arts of turning, chasing and inlaying.

motive behind the hanging of the paintings or in the arrangement of the glassware; the only consideration is compatibility. In a light English birch bureau the sombre Tula silverware glows softly and a set of coloured porcelain and some superb mediaeval ivories introduce a note of colour in contrast to the almost black hues of the silverware. A precious fifteenth-century *millefiori* glass piece from Venice is surrounded by pitchers and translucent glasses which endlessly reflect the rainbow created by the master glass makers of Venice. It is a private symphony where secret chords are struck between the objects.

Mikhail Perchenko has a genius for using space. Rows of miniatures hang under portraits with heavy gilt frames and echo the same theme in a minor chord. The symmetrical arrangement of five Dutch panels depicting low life is subtly interrupted by three little ivories and the oval of an earthenware dish. The collection is orchestrated like a musical score, betraying the owner's earlier vocation. His taste for crystal and porcelain is probably largely due to the musicality of their materials. Among these fragile treasures which resonate to the touch and are set alight by the slightest ray of light, are some outstanding opalines from Prince Marzov's private

222

20

These shelves house a set of cups depicting subjects based on well-known scenes from Russian literature. They come from the best factories in Russia: Gardner, Popov, the imperial Factory in St Petersburg and the private workshops of Prince Yusupov. Here the serfs added family portraits to the half-finished products imported from France, depicting genre scenes inspired by the paintings.

21 - 22

In the china cabinets and on the walls, porcelain and glassware of mixed provenance lend a note of colour to the pale poplar and Baltic pine Russian furniture and the chiaroscuro of an Italian Madonna and child.

224

23·24

A series of unsigned paintings on wood in the manner of Adriaen van Ostade (1610–1685) illustrate life in seventeenth-century Holland: genre scenes, romantic interiors, cabaret scenes, debauched peasants. RIGHT despite their caricature-like crudeness, the figures stand out from the dark grey background with a light, warm chiaroscuro.

workshops and the red and blue glassware destined for Count Orlov's table. These great aristocratic families owned factories that worked exclusively for them.

In addition to these fragile vestiges of the era of the boyars, there is porcelain ware from other places: Rouen, Delft, China and Meissen. Perchenko's all-consuming ambition is to recreate the refined life-style of the greatest periods in European history. He is fascinated by the Italian Renaissance. The most impressive piece in his collection is indisputably a magnificent Renaissance table adorned with foliage and fruit whose flat top is supported by winged chimerae and satyrs. It is sturdy without being inelegant, like the fine set of bronzes from the same period, also belonging to the collector. Most of them come from the St Petersburg palace of Prince Naryshkin, who, in the eighteenth century, was the Tsar's ambassador to Constantinople.

Over the centuries, kindred spirits are united by common taste. The ambassador prince and the contemporary Moscow collector have both revived the Italian tradition of the *cognoscenti*, those enlightened Renaissance art lovers who collected treasures in their cabinets of curiosities. For them, the possession of rare works of art was not a visible sign of wealth but the starting-point for a rigorous and refined life style. This Renaissance table, whose plain top is supported by sensual, mythological figures, illustrates this desire to combine epicureanism and austerity. This was the philosophy of the courts of Urbino and Ferrara which Balthasar Castiglione recorded in his treatise *The Courtier*. This is the spiritual family that Mikhail Perchenko feels he belongs to. He believes in a life of liberty, and is anxious to combine a sense of reality with the highest intellectual pursuits. Everything about him bears witness to such aspirations.

Dinner is served on an embroidered Venetian linen tablecloth. Beside the precious plates, the ruby facets of the glasses reflect the flames of the candles brought back from a recent trip to western Europe. There is no point trying to find any in Moscow. The candlesticks are by Germain and date from the eighteenth century. Meanwhile, the *pirozhkis* are served on seventeenth-century Chinese plates, as a famous Bordeaux vintage is uncorked.

All this is far removed from the shortages of Moscow. But Mikhail Perchenko has worked hard to fulfil his ambitions and achieve such elegance. He has adopted the relentless pace of a businessman from Paris, London or New York. Such drive is still surprising, even in the Russia of today. Mikhail Perchenko wants to pass on this energy and pragmatism to his son and is thinking of sending him to Tübingen, in Germany, where the strict Protestant education will prepare him for self-improvement without

sacrificing his individuality, which is the converse of the concept of education in the former USSR.

Caressing an Italian bronze or taking a mediaeval German ivory casket from a display cabinet, the collector freely quotes his favourite philosopher, Nietzsche from whom he borrowed his ideal 'superman', capable of reconciling Dionysian vitality and Apollonian elegance. The passion for possession, which brings a gleam to Mikhail Perchenko's eyes when he points out the finest pieces of his collection, is tempered by his concern for harmony in the arrangement of his treasures, and by his commitment to hard work. He goes to great lengths to find out more about the objects he buys and does not hesitate to enlist the assistance of eminent specialists when necessary. His curiosity knows no bounds and despite the constraints, his entrepreneurial spirit is always alert.

25 - 26
Collection of plates, platters, bottles, urns and Japanese vases from the Edo period (1603–1868). The polychrome floral decoration is inspired by a mixture of eighteenth-century Chinese motifs and western tastes.

Now, he wants to give his collection the space it deserves. His apartment is too small to house so many wonders, some of which have been placed in storage in the city. He thought of buying the roof of the house next door, raising it, pulling down the partition wall and thus creating an extension. Mikhail Perchenko is someone who is constantly extending his horizons. He has no illusions about the invasion of auction houses in post-communist Russia and he thinks that the country is in danger of being emptied of its artistic treasures without benefiting from the establishment of a proper market.

Meanwhile, the collector, faithful to an old habit, devotes one day a week to his passion. From five o'clock in the morning he is at one of the capital's flea markets, helping unpack the goods. The unfortunate vendor has to pay the price of ignorance if Perchenko walks off with a bargain: a rare piece of Meissen porcelain or a glass engraved with imperial figures. He thinks that those who are unable to appreciate the true value of these treasures do not deserve to keep them. This may seem to be rather a ruthless attitude, but it is fairly typical of the mentality of the contemporary boyars, in a country fraught with the most terrible contradictions.

27

A lidded vase in pastel tones, a vase with tapering sides,
a bottle, plates and an elephant, all nineteenth century,
from China and Japan.

28
Chinese monk, seventeenth century.
Indian ink drawing on rice paper.
150 x 65 cm approx.

230

29 - 30

Two plates from a collection of faience from the North, dating from the early eighteenth century.

31

European-style decorated plate from the Qianlong (Ch'ien-lung) period, eighteenth-century China, made in the Netherlands.

232

32 - 33

Italian Renaissance furniture which once belonged to Prince L.K. Naryshkin. The Roman Cartibulum was a model for this table adorned with wreaths, foliage, fruit and flowers, whose top is supported by winged chimerae.

34

Cabinet, probably from the Po valley, in walnut with light fruit tree inlay. The construction of this double front made of columns, gothic-style capitals, caryatids and satyrs, is clearly inspired by Palladian architecture.

THE MOSCOW BANK COLLECTION

234

1

Vyascheslav Ulupov is the President of the Moscow Bank. This forty-year-old man's meteoric climb up the social ladder reflects a country in a state of upheaval. A humble worker, he took up economics at Moscow University and, after obtaining a doctorate, was appointed director of the Stojkreditbank in 1990. Economic expansion and the more open attitude towards the West gave him the opportunity to build up a collection of contemporary art for the Moscow Bank, using western patronage as a model.

Vyacheslav Ulupov is the president of the Moscow Bank and belongs to the new generation of Russian collectors. The story of his success is exemplary. He was born in 1952 in Petropavlovsk-Kamchatsky, on the eastern borders of Russia and served in the army as a helicopter mechanic. His self-motivation drove him to take up economics at Moscow University, where he obtained a doctorate. At the beginning of 1990, he was appointed director of the Stojkreditbank. At the end of the year, when the Moscow Bank was set up, with a capital of more than a hundred million rubles, he became president. In 1991, it realized profits of 24 per cent, taking into account the rate of inflation. Ulupov decided then to build up a collection of contemporary art based on the western model, which would be owned by the Bank. To achieve this, he consulted specialists and brought in experts: Valeri Turchin,

professor of contemporary art history at Moscow University, Ekaterina Degot, from the Tretyakov Gallery, Ilya Sensiper, critic on the weekly *Ogoniok*, Pavel Khorchilov, Georgy Nikich and Inna Krimova.

Guided by his advisors, Vyacheslav Ulupov has surrounded himself with the best works by contemporary Russian painters. He is dependent on his mentors as art education is still sadly neglected in Russia and although many people are very well read, true art connoisseurs are very rare. The situation is gradually improving thanks to the determination of a few eminent figures inspired by the West.

Ulupov's six advisors are the founders of the first Moscow contemporary art fair, Art MIF (Moscow Art Fair), which was held in October 1990. This event was the signal the contemporary art

2

Griffons, 1989. *Natalya Nesterova.*
Oil on canvas. 170 x 280 cm

world in Russia had eagerly been awaiting. Between the 1990 Fair and that of 1991, seventy galleries opened their doors in Moscow. Suddenly, artists were being openly exhibited and a market was being created.

In the Moscow Bank collection, new artists from St Petersburg such as Timur Novikov and the Ukranian avant-garde represented by Alexander Roitburd, Arsen Savvodov, Georgy Senchenko and Oleg Golossiy can be found side by side with semi-official artists from the left wing of the former Union of Russian Artists which was disbanded in 1990. The most interesting of these painters is indisputably Vladimir Brainin, who has already been shown in France. He was born in 1951 and lives in Moscow. His paintings evoke a ghost town where huge black cars belonging to faceless party officials glide, where frescos are fading on the façade

of a house and only the statues seem to be alive. Brainin continuously repeats and builds on this vision, which, he says, came to him one day by chance: 'I was dozing on the back seat of the car and on waking up I suddenly saw a fantastic image out of the window: a strange town. It was unrecognizable but there was no doubt it was mine. Wonders can be seen all around us, in the falling rain, houses, cars and puddles. And behind all that, the Earth, Water, History, Life.' Through this dream landscape, Vladimir Brainin is trying to reach the essential existential truths. This desire to create a modern mythology is what artists as different as V. Brainin, Dimitri Krymov or Tatiana Nazarenko, all represented in Vyacheslav Ulupov's collection, have in common. Dimitri Krymov, who was born in 1954, draws on ancestral religious imagery and integrates it into the recent past. His 'wailing

236

3 **4**

The Magi, 1991. The Hare Cabin, 1990.
Dimitri Krymov. Sergei Shutov.
Oil on canvas. 124 x 150 cm. Mixed paints. 200 x 300 cm.

238

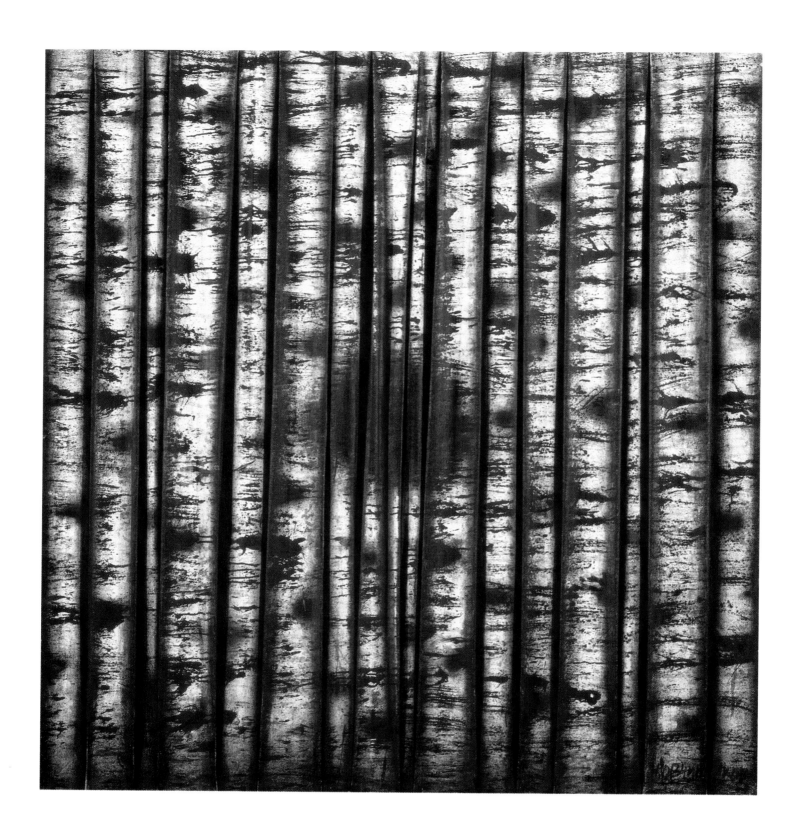

5
Six, *1990.*
Nikolai Ovchinnikov.
Oil on canvas. 200 x 190 cm.

wall', erected at the beginning of *Perestroika* in Moscow, celebrated the memory of the victims of Stalinism. Hundreds of photographs and mementos are plastered over this monument like a tragic jigsaw puzzle, and when there was no more room, people pinned photographs to their chests and stood there. Krymov evokes Biblical themes and uses collage techniques with rare genius: subjects cut into shreds, photographic montages and ink drawings, a shower of paper scraps from which an angel emerges, the mute expression of the despair of an anguished world in search of unity. Nothing could be further from the inspiration of Tatiana Nazarenko, whose *Country Life* is owned by the Moscow Bank. Here the colours contrast with the realities of peasant life and satirize Socialist Realism which prevailed until recent years. And

yet there is no trace of naivety in these portraits of country folk against a background of brightly coloured little houses. The models looking straight out of the canvas and the vivid imaginary colours lend the very human portraits the mystery of icons, giving these peasants the static dignity of the saints and angels painted centuries earlier. Whereas the aforementioned artists all belonged to the Union of Russian Artists which guaranteed them a minimum degree of freedom and comfort, Maksim Kantor was an outcast. His emaciated, tormented figures consumed by despair were considered too negative. His *Laocoon*, today owned by the Moscow Bank, gives mythological figures the sinister resignation of prisoners of the Gulag. The three men's massive, inert hands, rest in front of them in an admission of total helplessness and resignation.

239

6
Country Life, *1989.*
Tatiana Nazarenko.
Oil on canvas. 150 x 160 cm.

7 - 8

The entire Moscow Bank collection is locked away in vaults, with the exception of a few paintings which are reserved for the private enjoyment of their patron. Does this mean that for the new Russian collectors art is no more than a jealously guarded exchange currency? And yet, there is a glimmer of hope: we have recently learned that Vyacheslav Ulupov has agreed to lend the paintings for an exhibition which is to tour Russia.

Vyacheslav Ulupov not only represents the artistic tastes of the new enlightened bourgeoisie, he also embodies the radical metamorphosis of the art collecting profession in Russia. The works assembled remain constantly under lock and key, not for fear of the demands of the authorities, but of those of the criminal mafia whose activities have multiplied since the advent of *Perestroika*. Bank strong-rooms have replaced old-fashioned apartments hidden away in sordid inner courtyards. It is a good thing that indisputable masterpieces are being protected, but one cannot help wondering about their fate. Are they destined to serve as currency one day? Will speculation gain the upper hand? Let us hope not. Besides, Vyacheslav Ulupov has agreed to loan the Moscow Bank's paintings for a touring exhibition. It is safe to assume that as they travel up and down Russia, the works brought together by Vyacheslav Ulupov will themselves influence a new generation of artists.

241

9
Laocoon, *1991. Maksim Kantor.*
Oil on canvas. 100 x 120 cm.

Biographies of Russian artists

ALTMAN, NATAN ISAYEVICH
(1889–1970)
After studying at the Odessa Art Institute (1903–7), he attended M. Vasilyev's Free Russian Academy in Paris between 1910 and 1911. Before 1917, he exhibited Cubo-Futurist works in Russia, including the famous *Portrait of Anna Akhmatova*. He exhibited at the Futurist exhibition 'Tramway V' in Petrograd in 1915.

ANNENKOV, YURI PAVLOVICH
(1889–1974)
He studied in St Petersburg from 1908 to 1909 in the studio of S. Zaidenberg, then in Paris 1911–912 under Maurice Denis and Félix Valloton. His works were exhibited in Berlin (1922), in Venice (1924) and in Paris (1925).

AYVAZOVSKY, IVAN KONSTANTINOVICH
(1817–1900)
This painter was a pupil at the Academy of St Petersburg, then studied under Philippe Tanneur. He taught himself by copying the paintings of Joseph Vernet at the Hermitage Museum. At the age of twenty, his seascapes had assured his reputation. Three years later, he went on a long trip around Europe, visiting Italy, Holland, England and Spain. He returned to Russia in 1844 and enjoyed considerable renown in artistic circles. Appointed a member of the St Petersburg Academy, he participated in the Exhibition of 1900 in Paris with a painting called *The Ocean*.

BOGOMAZOV, ALEXANDER KONSTANTINOVICH
(1880–1930)
Having studied at Kiev Art School with A.

Ekster, he brought out, in 1914, a book on art theory: *Elements of Painting* (Elementy Zhivopisi), only a few extracts of which were published in the catalogue for 'The Ring' exhibition, which he organized with A. Ekster in Kiev. Bogomazov's artistic language falls somewhere between Laryonov's Rayonism and Italian Futurism. He designed decorations for public squares and propaganda parades from 1917. Then, in 1922, he became a professor at the Kiev Institute of Plastic Arts.

BURLYUK, DAVID DAVIDOVICH
(1895–1967)
Painter, poet and theoretician of Ukrainian extraction, he was the key figure behind Russian Futurism, along with Laryonov. He organized public debates, published almanacs and collections of poetry and was highly provocative, both verbally and in the way he dressed. He used literature and painting to promote the spread of Futurist propaganda throughout the Russian empire and even abroad (he was published in *Der Blaue Reiter* (The Blue Rider) in Munich in 1912). His articles on Cubism in the manifesto *A slap in the face of public taste* were a major landmark in the development of twentieth-century visual art theory.

CHAPIRO, JACQUES
(1887–date of death unknown)
He studied at the Kiev Art School then, from 1919, ran two art schools in Dnepropetrovsk and painted murals for the State. In 1920, he was head of a children's school, continuing his studies at the Petrograd (St Petersburg) Academy. In 1921, he designed Constructivist decor for Meyerhold's Theatre in Moscow. From 1925, he lived in Paris and participated in numerous exhibitions.

CHEKHONIN, SERGEI VASILYEVICH
(1878–1936)
From 1896–87, he studied at the Drawing School of the Society for the Encouragement of Arts in St Petersburg. In 1904, he worked in the Abrametsevo pottery workshop and exhibited at 'The World of Art'. In 1914, he participated in the Leipzig International Graphic Art and Book exhibitions. In 1928, he appeared with Falk, Altman and Vychegyanin at the Hirondelle gallery and at the salon in the rue de la Paix. Artistic director of the State Ceramics Factory in Petrograd, he was also head of a school of enamel painting in Rostov from 1925 to 1927, before settling finally in Paris in 1928.

CHUPYATOV, LEONID TERENTYEVICH
(1890–1942)
In 1909, he studied at the Drawing School of the Society for the Encouragement of Arts in St Petersburg. After a period in the studio of Tsionglinsky in 1912, he studied under M.Bernshteyn in 1916. He then continued his training in the Free Workshops in Petrograd under Petrov-Vodkin from 1918 to 1921. From 1926 to 1928, he taught at the Kiev Art Institute.

EKSTER ALEXANDRA ALEXANDROVNA
(1882–1949)
Until 1907, she attended the Kiev Art School where, in 1908, she organized 'The Link' exhibition with David Burlyuk. In Paris, she moved in Cubist circles and was influenced by Léger, then Ardengo Soffici. In Russia, she exhibited in many avant-garde shows between 1909 and 1924, the date of her final departure from Russia. She remains one of the major exponents of Fauvism, Cubism, Russian Cubo-Futurism and Constructivism.

FALK, ROBERT RAFAELOVICH
(1881–1958)
He studied in Moscow at the studios of K. Yuon and I. Mashkov. In 1910, he founded the Knave of Diamonds and was one of the most faithful exponents of Cézanne's legacy. As a member of the World of Art in 1911, he was influenced by Derain and Vlaminck. Between 1925 and 1928, he was a member of the Society of Moscow Artists and of the Association of Artists of Revolutionary Russia (AKhRR).

FILONOV, PAVEL NIKOLAEVICH
(1883–1941)
After his expulsion from the Academy of Arts in St Petersburg in 1910, he participated in the 'Union of Youth' exhibitions. From 1911, he travelled around Italy and France. On his return, between 1912 and 1915, he created large-scale canvases such as *The Cowgirls*, *The Feast of the Kings* and *Peasant Family*. He painted two backcloths for the play by V. V. Mayakovsky, *Vladimir Mayakovsky, Tragedy*. After illustrating Khlebnikov's collection of poetry, *Idols of Wood*, he published his first manifesto, *Made paintings* (Sdelannye kartiny), in which he drew up the principles of an 'analytical method'. Actively involved in his country's political upheavals, he participated in the first National Exhibition of Art in 1919, with a series of twenty-five paintings grouped under the title *Introduction to Universal Upheaval*. From 1925 onwards, he was head of the department studying ideologies (development of a synthetic theory based on the study of materials and on reports from other departments) at the National Institute of Artistic Culture in Leningrad. This department was to see the emergence of the Collective of Masters of Analytical Art (MAI), also called the Filonov School.

FYODOROV, GERMAN VASILYEVICH
(1885–1972)
This painter, who was also a graphic artist, studied at the Moscow School of Painting, Sculpture and Architecture. He participated in exhibitions including the World of Art and the Association of Artists of Revolutionary Russia. He taught at the Higher Technical-Artistic Studios and, in 1928, became a member of the Society of Moscow Artists.

GONCHAROVA, NATALIA SERGEEVNA
(1881–1962)
Having studied history, zoology and botany, Natalia Goncharova was admitted, in 1898, to the Moscow School of Painting, Sculpture and Architecture, where she met Laryonov. In 1906, she participated in the Exhibition of Russian Art in Paris, organized by Diaghilev as part of the Salon d'Automne. In 1907, she exhibited at the 'Stephanos' exhibition, which was the first showing of what was soon to be called the twentieth-century Russian avant-garde, and the following year she participated in the first Golden Fleece exhibition. In 1910, with Lentulov and Laryonov, she organized the first show by the Knave of Diamonds group in Moscow. Having founded the Donkey's Tail group, between 1911 and 1912, with Laryonov, in 1913 she organized 'The Target' exhibition which introduced some Rayonist works, the first attempt at abstract art in Russia. At the same time, she created the first Futurist book-objects, participated in the first German exhibition in the *Der Sturm* gallery and called for a return to the formal and thematic sources of Russian popular art. After 1919, she collaborated with Diaghilev in Paris, designing stage sets for ballets such as Stravinsky's *Firebird*.

GRIGORYEV, BORIS DMITRIEVICH
(1886–1939)
This painter and graphic artist studied under D. Shcherbinovsky at the Stroganov Institute between 1903 and 1907, and at the St Petersburg Academy between 1907 and 1912. In 1908, he exhibited typical subjects from Russian folklore, treated in a modernist way, at the Impressionist Exhibition, and from 1913, he exhibited at Mir Izkusstva, a club to which he belonged. He became professor at the Stroganov Institute in 1918, then left Russia for Berlin, where he published monographs such as *Russian Eroticism*. He arrived in Paris in 1929, studied the Apache world and worked for journals such as *Satirikon* and *Novy Satirikon* (New Satyricon). Several of the Expressionist works he exhibited in Moscow in 1918 went to the Russian Museum of St Petersburg and the Tretyakov Gallery in Moscow, as well as to the Museums of Modern Art in Paris and Venice.

KANDINSKY, VASILY VASILYEVICH
(1866–1944)
After studying law, he worked in Munich under Azbe and F. Von Stuck and founded his own school; his contributions to the journals *Die Neue Künstlervereinigung* and *Der blaue Reiter* made him one of the engineers of the artistic revival in Munich. His links with Russia were so strong, however, that it is impossible to separate his work from the history of Russian art. Kandinsky is one of the most eminent figures to have acted as a bridge between Russia and the West. Between 1910 and 1911, he published his first theoretical text called 'Concerning the Spiritual in Art' in an almanac. This text established for the first time the principle of 'inner necessity'. He exhibited at the Knave of Diamonds exhibition in 1910, translated a text by David Burlyuk on contemporary Russian painting into German, and by the distribution of countless reproductions introduced Russian woodcuts, *luboks*, to a wider audience. He played an active role in the artistic life of Russia during the early years of the Revolution. His theories, which were often assimilated into German Expressionism, made a profound impact on Russian artists and their growing awareness of the autonomy of artistic creation.

KANTOR, MAKSIM
(b.1957)
He lives in Moscow, and studied at the Institute of Printing from 1975 to 1980. Since 1982, he has exhibited in Russia, Japan, the United States and in Germany. In 1987, he participated in two exhibitions: 'Terror and Hope – Artists's view of peace and wartime' in Munich and 'The Mockba scene: four artists, four positions' in Berlin.

KLYUNKOV, IVAN VASILYEVICH, otherwise KLYUN
(1873–1942)
This Russian avant-garde painter, sculptor and theoretician studied art in Warsaw and Kiev. After 1905, he attended the studios of Fiodor Roerberg and Mashkov in Moscow. He had a great affinity with Malevich, and was one of the leading exponents of Suprematism, exhibiting at all the major Russian Futurist shows between 1913 and 1919, including 'The Union of Youth' and

'Tramway V'. In 1914, his style underwent a considerable change: he created sculpture-paintings closer to Archipenko's reliefs than to Tatlin's counter reliefs. He used collage as a base which he enlivened with painted woods, metal components and porcelain. His art bears the mark of decorative aesthetics and Symbolist philosophy. At the end of the twenties, he became the champion of French Purism and, some ten years later, of Surrealism.

KRYMOV, DIMITRI
(b.1954)
Born in Moscow, he studied art at the Moscow School of Art and Drama. In 1991, he participated in numerous Moscow exhibitions: The Dominus gallery's 'Paperworks', an exhibition of evangelical subjects at the Artist's Headquarters and at the Nina gallery.

KUZNETSOV, PAVEL VARFOLOMEEVICH
(1878–1968)
He studied art in Moscow. To combat the academicism which prevailed at the turn of the century, he founded the Mir Izkusstva group, which gave birth to the Knave of Diamonds (out of which emerged the Russian Constructivist and Abstract School) and the Blue Rose (to which he belonged). During a trip to Paris, he discovered the work of Gauguin, which was to be a lasting influence on his own landscapes. His work falls into two distinct periods: *The Blue Fountains* until 1905 and oriental subjects.

LARYONOV, MIKHAIL FYODOROVICH
(1881–1964)
At the Moscow School of Painting, Sculpture and Architecture, where he studied between 1898 and 1910, he met Natalya Goncharova. After exhibiting Impressionist works in Moscow, St Petersburg, Paris in 1906 and with Burlyuk in 1907 and 1908, he formed the Neo-Primitivist movement in 1909. He drew inspiration from the daily life of little provincial towns. In 1911, he broke with the Cézannists of the Knave of Diamonds which he had co-founded with Burlyuk the previous year. Refusing to bring up the rearguard of

European art, he participated with Goncharova in the illustration of a Futurist book. He remains one of the founding fathers of total abstraction with Kandinsky, Malevich and Mondrian. In 1915, he left Russia to work with Diaghilev's Ballets Russes. The lush colours and variety of his stage scenery and costumes inspired by Russian folk art have left a permanent mark on the history of art.

LEBEDEV, VLADIMIR VASILYEVICH
(1891–1967)
Painter and graphic artist, he studied at Tito's studio in St Petersburg in 1909 and at the Academy of Arts from 1912 to 1916. From 1911 to 1917, he worked as an illustrator for the magazines *Galchonok* (Young Jackdaw), *Satirikon, Novy Satirikon* and *Argus*. He began exhibiting in 1912 and became a member of the Obmokhu avant-garde movement. He designed propaganda posters for the *Rosta Windows* and worked as Art Editor for *Ogiz*. He remains a famous illustrator of children's books.

LENTULOV, ARISTARKH VASILYEVICH
(1882–1943)
He studied at the N. Selvyorstov Art College in Penza from 1898 to 1900, at the Kiev Art School under N. Pimonenko from 1900 to 1904, then at D. Kardovsky's School in St Petersburg from 1907 to 1908. He also studied under Le Fauconnier in Paris. He started out as an Impressionist, then came under the influence of Cézanne from 1909. A member of the Knave of Diamonds, he practised a Cézannism with daring distortions using an extremely violent Fauvist range of colours. From 1916 and until 1930, he designed stage scenery in Moscow. He taught at various art colleges, including the Free Workshops, the Moscow Institute of Fine Arts and the Higher Artistic and Technical Institute. He became a member of Obmokhu in 1919, of the Association of Painters of Revolutionary Russia in 1926 and of the Society of Moscow Artists in 1928.

LISSITZKY, LAZAR MARKOVICH
(1890–1941)
After studying architecture and engineering at

the Technical College in Darmstadt, he obtained his diploma in engineering in Riga in 1916. He then began his career as a painter, illustrating books, in particular the *Haggadah* in Yiddish. In 1917, he participated in 'The World of Art' exhibition. In 1919, he taught at the Art College in Vitebsk and worked with Chagall and Malevich who were a great influence on him. This was when he produced his first *Proun* paintings. In 1922, he published the journal *Vechtch/Gegenstand/ Object* in Berlin with Ilya Ehrenburg. Having abandoned painting in 1925, he supervised the design of the Soviet pavilion at the International Exhibition in Cologne from 1928. In 1930, he designed the pavilion at the Hygiene Exhibition in Dresden. The following year, he was the artist-architect responsible for the permanent Building Exhibition in Gorky Park. He was one of the guiding lights of Suprematism.

MALEVICH, KASIMIR SEVERINOVICH
(1878–1935)
In 1905, he settled in Moscow, where he studied at the School of Painting, Sculpture and Architecture. He sporadically exhibited works which showed Impressionist, Modern Style and even Symbolist tendencies. In 1910, he was invited by Laryonov to participate in the first Knave of Diamonds exhibition, with a series of Fauvist Neo-Primitive gouaches influenced by Gauguin, Matisse, Pre-Cubism and the *lubok*. Provincial and rural primitivism was succeeded by the various stages of Cubo-Futurism: geometric Cézannism, synthetic Cubism then the explosion of Suprematism in painting at the end of 1915, with the last Futurist exhibition, '0.10' in Petrograd (St Petersburg), with works such as the icon *Quadrangle* and the famous *Black square*. He staged Matiushin's opera *Victory over the Sun* and designed the scenery and costumes. In 1916, he formed the group Supremus. Suprematist philosophy and practices were to dominate the twenties, in opposition to Constructivism.

MASHKOV, ILYA IVANOVICH
(1881–1944)
After studying at the Moscow School of Painting, Sculpture and Architecture, he travelled to Europe in 1908 and participated

in exhibitions including 'The World of Art', 'Izdebsky's Salon' and the 'New Society of Artists'. A founder member of the Knave of Diamonds, he taught at the Higher Artistic and Technical Institute. From 1924 to 1932, he was a member of the Association of Painters of Revolutionary Russia.

NAZARENKO, TATIANA
(b.1944)
In 1968, she studied under A. Gritsay and D. Chilinsky at the Art Institute of Moscow. Then, from 1968 to 1972, she followed courses at the USSR Art Academy. She exhibited in 1987 in Leverkusen then in 1988 in Bremen. In 1978, she participated in the exhibition 'Three generations of three Muscovite (women) artists'.

NESTEROVA, NATALIA
(b.1944)
From 1955 to 1962, she studied at the Moscow Art School, then from 1962 to 1966 under A. Gritsay and Chilinksy at the Surikov Art Institute in Moscow. Since 1966, she has exhibited in the former USSR, in Bulgaria, in Germany, in Romania and in Poland.

NIVINSKY, IGNATI IGNATYEVICH
(1881–1933)
Painter, stage-designer and etcher, he studied at the Stroganov Institute in Moscow. *Blue Stones*, one of the artist's highly stylized etchings, appeared at the Exhibition of Russian Art in Paris in 1967.

OSMYORKIN, ALEXANDER ALEXANDROVICH
(1892–1953)
After studying at the Art School in Kiev from 1909 to 1911 and at the studio of Mashkov in Moscow from 1912 to 1913, he participated in exhibitions including 'The Knave of Diamonds', 'The World of Art' and 'Free Art'. He taught at the Leningrad Academy of Arts from 1932 to 1937.

OVCHINNIKOV, NIKOLAI
(b.1958)
Born in Moscow, he studied at the Art School there before settling in Paris. He exhibited at

the Kommunale Galerie in Frankfurt in 1988, at the Krings–Ernst Gallery in Cologne in 1989 and at the Galerie Froment & Putman in Paris in 1990.

PETROV-VODKIN, KUZMA SERGEEVICH
(1878–1939)
Painter, graphic artist and writer, he studied at the School of Painting and Drawing in Samara, then at the Central Stieglitz School and, in Paris, from 1905 to 1908. He then travelled to Italy, Greece, France and Africa. From 1906, he participated in exhibitions including 'The World of Art', 'Salon d'Automne' and 'The Golden Fleece'. He was the driving force behind the Symbolist movement in Petrograd where he was a teacher. He subsequently developed a form of mystic realism which treated subject matter and materials in a revolutionary way. He also left behind a literary oeuvre of which *The Woman of Samarkand, Khlynovsk* and *Prostranstvo Evklida* (Euclid's Space) are the best known works.

PIROSMANASHVILI, otherwise PIROSMANI, NIKOLAI ASLANOVICH
(1862–1918)
Georgian Naive painter, he was discovered by Futurists Ilya and Kirill Zdanevich and Le-Dentu who displayed his works at 'The Target' exhibition in 1913. Nicknamed 'The Russian Douanier Rousseau', he was self-taught as a painter and deeply influenced by the frescos of his homeland. He continued the oriental tradition of mural decoration, which accounts for the sheer size of his canvases. His favourite subjects were folk scenes and Georgian legends.

POPOVA, LYUBOV SERGEEVNA
(1889–1924)
She studied at the studios of Zhukovsky and Konstantin Yuon in Moscow from 1907 to 1908. Then she worked with Tatlin in the Tower studio. From 1914 to 1925, she participated in exhibitions including the Knave of Diamonds, '0.10', 'Tramway V', 'The Store' and '5x5=25'. Concentrating increasingly on the decorative arts, she illustrated books and created designs for

china and fabrics. In 1922, she designed the costumes and created the scenography for Meyerhold's production of Crommelynck's play *The Magnanimous Cuckold*. She participated in the first exhibition of Russian Art in the Diemen gallery in Berlin.

POUNI, IVAN ALBERTOVICH
otherwise POUGNY, JEAN
(1884–1956)
He studied at the Académie Julian in Paris from 1909 to 1910. On his return to St Petersburg in 1912, he participated in exhibitions including the 'Union of Youth', the 'Salon des Indépendants', 'Tramway V' and '0.10'. Co-author of the *Suprematist Manifesto* with Malevich he was invited to teach in Vitebsk from 1919. But he emigrated to Berlin in 1920, where he exhibited his works at the Der Sturm gallery. In 1923, he finally settled in Paris and took the name Jean Pougny.

RODCHENKO, ALEXANDER MIKHAILOVICH
(1891–1956)
He learnt his trade as an artist at the Art School in Kazan. He participated in Tatlin's exhibition, 'The Store', in Moscow in 1916. He was at that time greatly influenced by Malevich. In 1917, for the 'Café Pittoresque', staged by Yakulov, he created the designs for the Pre-Constructivist lamps. Three years later, he emerged as one of the leading exponents of Russian Constructivism.A founder member of Inkhuk, he and Kandinsky pioneered the setting up of a network of art museums throughout the country. In 1926, he collaborated on several Soviet film projects and, in 1930, he joined the October group.

RUKAVISHNIKOVA, VARVARA FYODOROVNA
(1878–1966)
Having studied porcelain painting from 1903 to 1908, she specialized in majolica. A porcelain painter and designer, she participated in 'The World of Art' exhibitions and the Peterhof National Engraving factory exhibition. She taught porcelain painting at the Factory school from 1946 to 1950.

SHEVCHENKO, ALEXANDER VASILYEVICH
(1882–1948)

Painter and theoretician, he learnt his profession at the Stroganov School of Decorative Arts in Moscow from 1897 to 1905. He studied at the studio of Eugène Carrière, then at the Académie Julien in Paris in 1905 and 1906 and, after 1907, under the Impressionist painter, K. Korovin, at the Moscow School of Painting, Sculpture and Architecture. Between 1910 and 1914, with Laryonov, he promoted the spread of Neo-Primitivism and in 1913 defined his ideas in a pamphlet. Between 1913 and 1914 he painted Cubo-Futurist works while remaining faithful, broadly speaking, to Cézannian Cubism.

SHTERENBERG, DAVID PETROVICH
(1881–1948)

He studied at the Ecole des Beaux Arts and at the Académie Witte in Paris. He participated in the Salon d'Automne and in the Salon des Indépendants. In 1917, he exhibited with Matisse, Ozenfant and Utrillo in Paris. On his return to Russia, he was appointed Commissar for the Arts. In 1922, he was in Berlin, where he participated with Altman and Chagall in the 'Exhibition of Three'. In 1925, he founded the Society of Easel Painters (OST), of which he was President until 1930.

SHUTOV, SERGEI
(b.1955)

Born in Potsdam, he now lives in Moscow. In 1986, he exhibited at the Mayakovsky Museum in the Russian capital and, in 1989, at the Katia Granoff gallery in Paris and at the Barbizon Gallery in Glasgow. In 1990, having exhibited at the Helen Drutt gallery in New York, he exhibited at the Dominus gallery in Moscow.

SOFRONOVA, ANTONINA FYODOROVNA
(1892–1966)

She studied at Roerberg's studio in Moscow from 1910 to 1913, and at Mashkov's studio from 1913 to 1914. From then onwards, she participated in exhibitions including the 'Knave of Diamonds', 'The World of Art' and 'MTKH'. She became a member of the Thirteen organization in 1931.

SUETIN, NIKOLAI MIKHAILOVICH
(1897–1954)

He studied at the Higher Art Institute in Vitebsk from 1918 to 1922 and joined the Unovis group. He started to exhibit in 1920. In 1923, he worked at the State Ceramics Factory, then from 1927 to 1930 at the experimental laboratory at the Institute of Art History. In 1932, he was chief artist at the artistic laboratory at the Leningrad Ceramics Factory. At the same time, he worked as an illustrator. A well-known Suprematist artist, he designed the Soviet pavilions at the World Exhibitions in Paris (1937) and New York (1939).

TATLIN, VLADIMIR YEVGRAFOVICH
(1885–1953)

From 1902 to 1910, he attended the Moscow School of Painting, Sculpture and Architecture and the Art College in Penza. From 1911 to 1914, he exhibited regularly and, in particular, with 'The Union of Youth' and the 'Donkey's Tail'. At these exhibitions, he showed figurative and neo-primitive works in which the firm outlines of the drawing are combined with simplicity of line and schematic construction. Laryonov's influence can be seen in the subjects taken from the world of work and folk tales. In 1914, in his Moscow studio, he showed his *Painting reliefs* which he was intending to exhibit the following year at 'Tramway V' in Petrograd. His *Angular reliefs* appeared at the last Futurist exhibition, '0.10'. In 1916, he organized 'The Store' exhibition. After the 1917 Revolution, he was regarded as the father of Constructivism.

TYSCHLER, ALEXANDER GRIGORYEVICH
(1886–1961)

From 1912 to 1917, he studied at the Kiev Art School, then attended the studio of A. Ekster between 1917 and 1919. In 1925, he became a member of the Society of Easel Painters (OST). From 1927, he designed stage scenery for the Jewish theatres in Minsk and in Kharkov and for the MGSPS theatre (of the Moscow town council of unions). He participated in the International Exhibitions of Dresden in 1926 and Leipzig in 1927 and 1928.

VEYSBERG, VLADIMIR GRIGORYEVICH
(1924–1985)

He studied at the studio of the Union in Moscow from 1943 to 1948 and in the studios of Mashkov and Osmyorkin. From 1956, he participated in the 'Exhibition of the Nine' in Moscow and the 'Exhibition of the Eight' in Leningrad. He had one-man shows in Paris in 1984 and in Moscow in 1987.

ZDANEVICH, KIRILL MIKHAILOVICH
(1882–1970)

He studied at the School of Painting and Sculpture in Tbilisi and in Paris from 1912 to 1914. He participated in exhibitions including the 'Donkey's Tail' and the 'Target' and worked in Tatlin's studio. It was he who discovered the naive Georgian painter Pirosmani. He illustrated Futurist poetry collections, especially those by Mayakovsky.

ZVEREV, ANATOLI
(b.1931)

He has painted since childhood, and entered the School of Art in Moscow, only to be expelled six months later for having painted a nude on the back of a portrait of Stalin which he had taken down from the wall. In 1957, he participated in the International Workshop of Plastic Arts at the 6th World Festival of Youth. He is regarded as a Fauvist artist among the ranks of the non-conformist painters in Moscow. He paints with anything on any surface, mixing both media and techniques as the inspiration takes him. He has already had exhibitions in Paris, New York, Geneva and Lugano.

INDEX

Page numbers in italics refer to illustrations.

	HISTORY		ARTISTIC LIFE	
	In Russia	**Outside Russia**	**In Russia**	**Outside Russia**
1917	February Revolution in Petrograd. Abdication of Nicholas II. October: success of the Bolshevik revolution.	The United States declare war on Germany.	Chagall is appointed Commissar at the Art School in Vitebsk.	Picabia publishes the periodical *391* and Reverdy publishes the periodical *Nord-Sud* (North-South).
1918	Beginning of the civil war. Peace treaty of Brest-Litovsk. Beginning of Communist War .	Armistice at Rethondes. Collapse of the Austro-Hungarian empire.	Poem by Blok: *The Twelve*. Malevich *White Square on White Background*.	Apollinaire and Poulenc: *Les Mamelles de Tirésias* (The Breasts of Tiresias). Mondrian: *Composition*: colour planes with grey lines.
1919		Treaty of Versailles. Foundation of the Republic of Weimar. Creation of the League of Nations.		The Bauhaus is created. Death of Auguste Renoir.
1920	Victory of the Red Army over Wrangel in the Crimea.		Dziga Vertov creates the first full-length newsreels.	Mondrian: doctrine of Neo-Plasticism. Matisse: costumes, decor for *Le Chant du Rossignol* by Stravinsky.
1921	Kronstadt mutiny. New Economic Policy (NEP) adopted.	Conviction of Sacco and Vanzetti in the United States. Chinese Communist Party founded.	Creation of the Russian Association of Proletarian Writers (RAPP). Kandinsky at the Bauhaus.	Einstein, Nobel Prize for physics. Duchamp launches the review *New York-Dada*.
1922	The Cheka becomes the GPU Stalin, secretary general of the Communist Party. Official constitution of the USSR.	Mussolini comes to power. Hitler publishes the first part of *Mein Kampf*.	Launch of *Lef* (left-wing art magazine). Chagall and Kandinsky leave Russia for Germany.	Monet: *Les Nymphéas* (Water Lilies). Joyce: *Ulysses*. In Paris, collapse of Dadaism. Death of Proust.
1923		Failure of Hitler's Munich *putsch*.	Creation of the Museum of Modern Art in Moscow. Archipenko settles in New York, Chagall and Pevsner in Paris.	
1924	Death of Lenin. 2nd Soviet Constitution adopted.	Olympic Games in Paris.		Breton: *Surrealist Manifesto*. Kandinsky, Feininger, Jawlensky and Klee form *Der Blaue Reiter* (*The Blue Rider*) group.
1925	Trotsky is excluded from the government.	China: National Revolution.	Eisenstein: *The Battleship Potemkin*. Suicide of Yesenin.	Paris: exhibition of Decorative Arts (Léger, Delaunay, Sue, Mare). First Surrealist exhibition.
1928	Beginning of first Five-Year Plan.		Exhibition of contemporary French painting in Moscow.	Breton *Surrealism and Painting*. Brecht and Weill: *The Threepenny Opera*. Buñuel and Dali: *Un Chien Andalou* (An Andalusian Dog)
1929	Trotsky is expelled from the USSR. Beginning of forced collectivization campaign.	Wall Street Crash. Lateran Treaties between the Vatican and the Fascist government.	Film by Dziga Vertov: *The Man with the Movie Camera*.	World Exhibition in Barcelona. Creation of the Museum of Modern Art in New York. Death of Diaghilev.
1930	Stalin publishes *Dizzy with Success* in *Pravda*. Mass trials for academics and engineers.		Closure of the Leningrad History of Art Institute. Suicide of Mayakovsky.	De Chirico: *Hebdomeros*. Vienna: exhibition of Contemporary Russian Art. Le Corbusier returns from the USSR.
1931	Anti-religious Five-Year Plan adopted. Internal passport for Soviet citizens re-introduced.	Spain: proclamation of the Republic.		Faulkner: *Sanctuary*. First International Exhibition of Architecture at the Museum of Modern Art in New York.
1932	Famines.	Assassination of French President, Paul Doumer.	Decree relating to the restructuring of artistic and literary organizations.	Kandinsky: *Reflecting on abstract art*. Dali: *Critical Paranoic*. Matisse: *Dance*.
1933	Inauguration of White Sea-Baltic canal.	Roosevelt, President of the United States. Hitler, German Chancellor.	Bunin, who has emigrated to France, receives the Nobel Prize for literature.	The Bauhaus is disbanded. The periodical, *Minotaur*, is published. Chicago: World Exhibition.
1934	The GPU becomes the NKVD (People's Comissariat of Internal Affairs). Admitted to the League of Nations.	Assassination of Dollfuss. Mao Tse-Tung's `Long March'. Night of the Long Knives in Munich.	Inaugural congress of the Union of Writers. Proclamation of Socialist Realism in literature.	Paris: exhibition of Realist painters. Pirandello: Nobel Prize for literature. Gropius takes refuge in London.
1936	Death of Gorky. First Moscow trial (fourteen defendants). Promulgation of the `Stalin' Constitution.	Spanish Civil War, General Franco becomes Caudillo. Anti-Comintern Pact (Germany-Japan).	Creation of the Committee of Artistic Affairs of the Council of Ministers of the USSR.	Gershwin: *Porgy and Bess*. Picasso: *Guernica*. Paris: *Formes Nouvelles* (new forms) exhibition.

	HISTORY		ARTISTIC LIFE	
	In Russia	**Outside Russia**	**In Russia**	**Outside Russia**
1937	Second Moscow trial (seventeen defendants including Pyatakov and Radek). Trial and execution of Tukhachevsky.	Japan invades China.	Mukhina: `The Worker and the Woman Collective Farmer', sculpture for the Soviet pavilion at the International Exhibition.	Paris: International Exhibition. Munich: exhibition of degenerate art and of new German art.
1938	Third Moscow trial. (Bukharin, Rykov, Rakovsky, Yagoda).	Hitler annexes Austria (*Anschluss*). Crystal Night. Munich Agreement over the Sudetenland.	Death of Mandelstam in a concentration camp. *Alexander Nevsky*, film by Eisenstein, music by Prokofiev.	Paris: Exhibition `L'art sacré moderne' (Modern Sacred Art). Surrealist Exhibition. Film by M. Carné: *Quai des Brumes* (Port of Shadows).
1939	Nazi-Soviet Pact. Partition of Poland. Outbreak of Soviet-Finnish war.	Outbreak of the Second World War. End of the Spanish Civil War.		Picasso exhibition at the Museum of Modern Art in New York. First Exhibition of New Realities.
1940	Assassination of Trotsky. Baltic states and Bessarabia annexed. Absenteeism from work regarded as an offence.	Appeal by General de Gaulle on BBC Radio. Rethondes Armistice.		Artists emigrate to the United States. Hemingway: *For Whom the Bell Tolls*. Chaplin: *The Great Dictator*.
1941	Hitler invades the USSR. Seige of Leningrad begins. German army stopped outside Moscow.	Pearl Harbour: The United States enter the war.		Duchamp: *Boîte en valise*.
1942	Soviet offensive outside Stalingrad.	Americans begin landing in North Africa.	*Ivan The Terrible*, film by Eisenstein, music by Prokofiev (second part not shown until 1958).	Mondrian: *Broadway Boogie-Woogie*. New York: exhibition *Artists in Exile*. Paris: opening of Museum of Modern Art.
1943	German surrender at Stalingrad. Battle of Kursk. Re-establishment of Patriarchate: election of Sergei.	Fall of Mussolini. Surrender of Italy. Comintern dissolved. Teheran Conference.		First Pollock exhibition in New York. Sartre: *L'Etre et le Néant* (Being and Nothingness).
1944	End of siege of Leningrad. Red Army enters Bucharest, Sofia, Belgrade and Warsaw.	Allies land in Normandy. Liberation of Paris. Rome taken by the Allies.		First Dubuffet exhibition. First international exhibition of Concrete Art.
1945	Election of Patriarch Alexei.	Surrender of Germany. Surrender of Japan. Nuremburg trials. Yalta Conference. Creation of the UN.		New York: Mondrian Retrospective. Sartre founds the review, *Les Temps Modernes*. M Carné: *Les Enfants du Paradis* (Children of Paradise).
1946	People's commissariats are re-named `ministries': the NKVD becomes MVD (Ministry of Internal Affairs).	Nuremburg trials. Churchill's speech at Fulton (`Iron Curtain', start of the Cold War).	Decree passed by the Central Committee of the Communist Party regarding the periodicals *The Star* and *Leningrad*.	Paris: exhibition of Art Brut.
1947	Famine in the Ukraine. Cominform established.	Partition of Palestine. Expulsion of Communist ministers in France and in Italy. Independence of India.	The USSR Academy of Arts set up to cover all aspects of art education in the country.	Opening of the National Modern Art Museum in Milan. Camus: *La Peste* (The Plague). Gide: Nobel Prize for literature.
1948	The Russians blockade Berlin.	Communist take-over of Prague by force. Creation of the State of Israel. Assassination of Gandhi.		*Arte Astratta* in Italy. Foundation of the Cobra movement. De Sica: *Bicycle Thieves*.
1949	First Atomic Bomb.	Creation of NATO (North Atlantic Treaty Organization). Creation of Comecon.		Orwell: *1984*. Picasso: *Dove of peace*.
1950	Sino-Soviet Pact.	Outbreak of the Korean war.		Le Corbusier: Ronchamps Church. Niemeyer builds Brasilia. Ionesco: *La Cantatrice chauve* (The Bald Prima Donna).
1953	Death of Stalin. The USSR announces its first H-bomb. Khrushchev, First Secretary of the Communist Party of the Soviet Union.	Rioting in East Berlin. Armistice in Korea.		Breton supports Abstract Expressionism. New York: `Young American Painters' at the Guggenheim Museum.
1954	The MVD becomes the KGB (State Security Committee).	French defeat of Dien Bien Phu in Vietnam. Geneva Agreements. Outbreak of the Algerian war.	Ehrenburg's novel: *The Thaw*.	The United States: development of Action Painting. Alloway uses the term Pop Art for the first time.
1955	Malenkov replaced. Bulganin and Khrushchev visit Yugoslavia.	Warsaw Pact is signed.	Pasternak finishes novel: *Doctor Zhivago*.	Elvis Presley: Rock'n'Roll. Kassel: *Dokumenta 1*, development of pictorial abstraction.

	HISTORY		ARTISTIC LIFE	
	In Russia	**Outside Russia**	**In Russia**	**Outside Russia**
1956	Soviet army invades Budapest. Khrushchev's secret speech at the 20th Party Congress.	Rioting in Poznan and East Berlin. Uprising in Budapest. Nationalization of the Suez Canal.	Novel by Dudintsev: *Not by Bread Alone*	First manifesto of Pop Art. Antonioni: *The Cry*.
1957	Zhukov removed. First man-made satellite from Earth: Sputnik 1.	Treaty of Rome, constitution of the EEC. Hungary: start of the trial for those involved in the Budapest uprising.	Pasternak's novel *Doctor Zhivago* is published abroad. Film by Kalatozov: *The Cranes are Flying*.	Camus: Nobel Prize for literature.
1958	Khrushchev is made President.	The Communist daily newspaper, *The Daily Worker*, folds in the United States. End of the Fourth Republic in France.	Pasternak refuses to accept the Nobel Prize for literature.	
1959	Khrushchev visits the United States.	Cuba: Fidel Castro comes to power, break with the United States. De Gaulle, President of the Fifth Republic.		Exhibition: `Jackson Pollock and New American Painting' at the Museum of Modern Art in Paris.
1960	Khrushchev at the UN General Assembly in New York. A rift opens between the USSR and China.	Foundation of OPEC. Olympic Games in Rome. Kennedy, President of the United States.	Death of Pasternak.	Milan: `Le Nouveau Réalisme'.
1961	Khrushchev meets Kennedy in Vienna. Gagarin is the first man in space.	Construction of the Berlin Wall begins. In the United States, the Communist party is outlawed.		Resnais and Robbe-Grillet: *Last year at Marienbad*. Foucault: *Histoire de la folie à lâge classique* (Madness and Civilization).
1962	USSR announces that it will supply arms and instructors to Cuba.	Cuban Missile Crisis. Battle of the Bay of Pigs. Evian Agreements: end of the Algerian war.	Start of the campaign against `liberal tendencies' in culture.	Release in Paris, after an eight-month ban, of *Viridiana*, a film by Luis Buñuel.
1963	Breakdown of Sino-Soviet relations. Castro in Moscow: first foreigner to receive the title of `Hero of the USSR'.	The `Hot Line', linking the White House and the Kremlin, is set up. Assassination of John F. Kennedy.		Inauguration of the Matisse Museum in Nice and the Picasso Museum in Barcelona. Death of Cocteau, Tzara and Braque.
1964	Brezhnev replaces Khrushchev.	The American Senate passes the Civil Rights Act for Negroes. Outbreak of war in Vietnam.	Death of Laryonov.	World Exhibition in New York. Chagall paints the ceiling of the Paris Opera House.
1965	Pact giving aid to Poland is signed.	Demonstration in the United States against the Vietnam war. Death of Winston Churchill.		André Masson Retrospective at the National museum of Modern Art in Paris. Death of Le Corbusier.
1966	Expulsion of all Chinese students. Communist Party condemns the Chinese cultural revolution. End of `thaw'.	Outbreak of the Cultural Revolution in China. General de Gaulle visits the USSR.	Death of Akhmatova. Film by Tarkovsky: *Andrei Rublev*.	Death of Alberto Giacometti and André Breton. Student unrest in the United States and Europe.
1967	Rehabilitation of Tartars from the Crimea. Kosygin visits Great Britain. Andropov, head of the KGB.	China is refused entry to the UN. Six-Day War in Israel. Assassination of Che Guevara.	Death of Ilya Ehrenburg.	World Exhibition in Montreal. Birth of Arte Povera and of Land Art. Death of Magritte.
1968	Military intervention in Czechoslovakia. Demonstration in Red Square (against this invasion).	May Events in Paris. Prague Spring crushed by Russian tanks. Olympic Games in Mexico.	Writer Anatol Kuznetsov gains right of asylum in Great Britain.	`The Art of the Real' in London, Paris, New York, Zurich. Bauhaus Exhibition in Paris. Death of Duchamp.
1969	Sino-Soviet confrontation. Formation of `action group' for the defence of civil rights in the USSR.	American astronauts, Aldrin and Armstrong, walk on the moon. Resignation of De Gaulle.		Pop Music Festival at Woodstock. Beckett, Nobel Prize for literature. Costa-Gavras: *Z*.
1970	Resumption of diplomatic relations with Peking. The cost of an exit visa for the West soars.	First meeting between the leaders of East and West Germany since the end of the war. S. Allende, President of Chile.	Tvardovsky has to leave `Novy mir'. Solzhenitsyn receives the Nobel Prize for literature.	`Expo 70' in Osaka. Support-Surface group.
1971	Start of a mass Jewish exodus to Israel. Election of Patriarch Pimen. Death of N. Khrushchev.	China allowed to enter UN.		Francis Bacon and Fernand Léger Retrospectives at the Grand Palais. Death of Igor Stravinsky.
1972	First SALT treaty signed in Moscow.	The Supreme Court of the U.S. rules that Death Penalty is unconstitutional. Terrorist attack at the Munich Olympic Games.		Film by Visconti: *Ludwig*. Scandal at the *72-72* exhibition in Paris. Heinrich Böll, Nobel Prize for literature.

	HISTORY		ARTISTIC LIFE	
	In Russia	**Outside Russia**	**In Russia**	**Outside Russia**
1973	Official visit by Brezhnev to Cuba.	Resignation of President Nixon after the scandal of the Watergate Affair. Yasser Arafat (PLO) invited to the UN.	Solzhenitsyn is expelled from the USSR. Shukshin's film: *The Red Snowball Tree*	Miró Exhibition at the Grand Palais. Milan Kundera: *Life is Elsewhere*. International success of Hyper-Realism.
1975	Sakharov, Nobel Peace Prize.	First Soviet-American space mission. Saigon falls into the hands of the Communists. Death of Franco.	Death of Shostakovich.	Milos Forman: *One Flew over the Cuckoo's Nest*. Lichtenstein Retrospective in Paris.
1976	Formation of groups to monitor the implementation of the Helsinki agreements in Moscow and in various republics.	Americans warn against allowing European Communist parties into power.	Ernst Neizvestny departs for the West.	*Russian Art in Exile* exhibition, from the Alexander Glezer collection, at the Palais des Congrès in Paris.
1977	`Brezhnev' constitution, IV Soviet constitution, adopted.	Deng Xiaoping back in power in China. Eurocommunism takes hold in Spain.		Inauguration of the Georges Pompidou National Centre for Art and Culture in Paris. Death of Charlie Chaplin and J. Prévert.
1978	Trial of Dr Y. Orlov, founder of the Group for monitoring the Helsinki agreements.	Tensions between East and West Germany. Camp David Talks.		*Paris-Berlin* exhibition at the Georges Pompidou Centre in Paris.
1979	Military intervention in Afghanistan.	Second SALT treaty signed between the United States and the USSR. Victory of the Islamic Revolution in Iran.	Death of Consta.	*Paris-Moscow* exhibition at the Georges Pompidou Centre in Paris.
1980	Sakharov is exiled to Gorky. Olympic Games in Moscow boycotted by the United States and their allies.	Lech Walesa's `Solidarity' movement wins support throughout Poland. Outbreak of Iran-Iraq war.		Exhibition *Les Réalismes 1919-1939* at the Georges Pompidou Centre.
1981	26th Party Congress.	EEC: European council of Maastricht. State of siege in Poland. Assassination of Anwar El-Sadat.	Film by Mikhalov: *Family Relations*. *Moscow-Paris* Exhibition at the Pushkin museum in Moscow.	Picasso's *Guernica* arrives in Madrid. International recognition of new German art.
1982	Death of Suslov. Death of Brezhnev, succeeded by Andropov at the head of the Communist Party.	China: 12th Communist Party Congress, new constitution. American-Soviet summit project.		Gabriel Garcia Marquez: Nobel Prize for literature. Death of Louis Aragon.
1984	Death of Andropov, succeeded by Chernenko. Talks resumed with the United States.	Assassination of Indira Gandhi. Multi-national forces pull out of Lebanon.	Tarkovsky goes into voluntary exile.	*Primitivism in Twentieth-Century Art* exhibition in New York.
1985	Death of Chernenko, succeeded by Gorbachev. Reagan-Gorbachev summit in Geneva. Perestroika. Glasnost.	Mexico devastated by an earthquake.		Death of Chagall, Dubuffet and Diego Giacometti.
1986	Nuclear disaster at Chernobyl. Failure of meeting at the Gorbachev-Reagan summit at Reykjavik.	China: students demonstrate for more freedom and democracy. Terrorist attacks in France.		Death of Jean Genet. Tarkovsky: *The Sacrifice*. Opening of the Picasso Museum at the Hôtel Salé in Paris.
1987	Gorbachev proposes election, with secret ballots for certain key Party posts.	Death penalty abolished in East Germany. Irangate scandal in the United States. Financial crash in Wall Street.	J. Brodsky, in exile in the United States, receives the Nobel Prize for literature. Chagall exhibition in Moscow.	*Arp 1886-1966* exhibition at the Paris Museum of Modern Art in Paris. Death of André Masson and Marguerite Yourcenar.
1988	Ministry of Foreign Affairs confirms the release of about 140 dissidents.	Agreements signed in Geneva on the withdrawal of Soviet troops from Afghanistan. End of Iran-Iraq war.	Publication of famous Samizdat works: Dombrovsky: *Faculty of uselessness*; Grossman: *Life and destiny*, etc.	Fellini's film: *Intervista*.
1989	First free elections	Chinese students on Tiananmen Square. Assassination of the Polish dictator, Ceauscescu. Fall of the Berlin Wall.	Union of Soviet Writers authorizes the publication of *The Gulag Archipelago* by Solzhenitsyn.	Filonov exhibition in Paris. I. M. Pei: The Louvre Pyramid. Death of Salvador Dali.
1990	The Baltic states declare their independence. Events in Vilnious, Riga and Tallin.	Reunification of Germany. East-West summit of the CSCE (Conference on Security and Co-operation in Europe) in Paris.	Death of the collector George Kostakis in Athens.	*Le Corps en morceau* (The body in pieces) exhibition at the Orsay Museum in Paris. Death of Philippe Soupault and Erté.
1991	August Putsch. End of the USSR, organization of the CIS. Yeltsin, President of Russia.	Gulf War. End of apartheid. Dissolution of the Warsaw Pact.		André Breton Exhibition in Paris. *Chagall in Russia* exhibition in Martigny (Switzerland).

PHOTOGRAPHY CREDITS